*Presented to*

_____

*By*

_____

*On the Occasion of*

_____

*Date*

_____

# WHAT I LEARNED
# FROM GOD WHILE...

# Cooking

Compiled and Edited by
## Cristine Bolley

BARBOUR
PUBLISHING

Published by Barbour Publishing, Inc., P.O. Box 719, Uhrichsville, Ohio 44683, www.barbourbooks.com

*Our mission is to publish and distribute inspirational products offering exceptional value and biblical encouragement to the masses.*

ecpa Member of the
Evangelical Christian
Publishers Association

Printed in the United States of America.
5 4 3 2 1

# Dedicated

To our grandmothers, who showed
us that the fellowship of a home-cooked
meal and the giving of thanks for our daily
bread are still the best gifts we can pass
to the next generation.

# Contents

# Cris's Appetizer

Here's Something You Should Know
before You Read This Cookbook.
(But if I called this the Editor's Preface,
you would probably skip this page.)

If cooking skills were genetic, I would be a master chef. My grandmother was a great cook who prepared meals for the prisoners in the county jail because Grandpa was the sheriff. And rumor has it that men committed crimes just to be incarcerated so they could eat her cooking! My sister, Vonda, tells the story in this book about the hundreds of cookies Grandma made each Christmas. She was the town baker long before commercial bakeries were opened in our small hometown.

As my children will confirm, I didn't inherit Grandma's cooking skills. When we told our daughters it was time for dinner, they ran for the car, calling out dibs on which restaurant they wanted to go to next. The first turkey I ever cooked still had the paper bag of giblets inside when we carved it, and my gravy flipped out of the pan like a pancake. In fact, I could fill a book with stories of good recipes gone bad, proving that it must have been the grace of God to have been chosen to edit this devotional.

I could also fill many pages trying to explain the awesome presence of God that I felt while reading and editing these stories. The fifty-two contributors of this work were not given a sample to follow. "Just write from your life experience," I told them. "Become your own favorite storyteller—but tell it in 350 words." I didn't even assign them a specific category of recipe to send—we just went "potluck." But is it surprising that there was a balanced number of entries between breakfast, breads, sides, entrées, and desserts? Or does it prove that the Lord is a Master Chef, who hand selects our balanced meals and watches over the process until it is just right?

If you can keep from reading this book in one sitting, you will find that it offers a devotion for each week of the year. I thought it was amazing when Lynn Morrissey's recipe for Pumpkin Pie Cake fell naturally on the week before Thanksgiving, just in time to add it to your menu each year! And six people wrote about the holidays, which was just the right number of stories to fill the weeks between Thanksgiving and Christmas!

The outcome of this book is evidence that the same Lord met each one of us as we looked to Him for solutions. From Ada Brownell's simple examination of an egg to Don Dilmore's elaborate explanation of how to make fruitcake, I believe that you, too, will see the parallels of how our faith can steadily expand from a tiny idea to a deep, rich treat if we continue to feed it the truth of God's wisdom.

I definitely see cooking in a different light after

reading these stories. In fact, I am eager to get back into my kitchen, throw out the old unused spices and renew its staples so that I will be ready if the Lord wants to talk to me in the kitchen again.

So what's the right expression here? Oh—*bon appétit!*

# Acknowledgments

I am grateful to the creative team at Barbour Publishing who believed this book should be added to this series and for sharing my vision of touching people with stories of God's presence in everyday events.

Thank you, Susan Schlabach, for birthing this series into production, right before birthing your own family into the world. Thank you, Kelly Williams, for picking up the vision and keeping the project going.

It was through the networking ability of Linda Evans Shepherd, founder of Advanced Writers and Speakers (AWSA), and Marita Littauer, president of Christian Leaders and Speakers Services (CLASServices), that I was able to find so many gifted writers to contribute to this work. And what a wonderful gift the two of you offer to the world by strengthening those who are called to proclaim God's good news.

And kudos to the contributors to this work. You were all amazing to work with. Your prompt response and insightful wisdom are evidence of your close walk with God. We will continue to learn from the stories that you plant in our hearts.

Thank you to my husband, James, who keeps the barbecue going when I'm pushing the last days of a book deadline. I'll cook tomorrow, sweetheart. Whatever you want, your choice, and here are fifty-two new recipes that I have learned how to do. . . .

# A Note from Cristine

I was a newlywed when I first understood that the task of cooking is more about the subsequent fellowship of sharing meals with others than its consequential nourishment of our bodies. As newcomers to New Zealand, my husband and I were frequently invited to dinner in the homes of our newly acquainted friends.

One day while living in Wellington, we decided to invite our Kiwi friends to a Tex-Mex dinner. Preparing that meal turned into an international event. Our parents mailed a bag of ground maize to us so we could make our own tortilla shells. I had learned to roll the tortillas from a Fijian friend who made similar bread called *rotis*. My husband and I spent an entire day preparing the food, and once we presented it to our guests, it disappeared within a few minutes. I thought then how futile the work had been, but I realize now that the memory of it has lasted more than thirty years, proving the effort wasn't in vain after all.

I don't know how many days my friend Yania spent preparing the meal she invited us to share. I met her while going door-to-door to meet my neighbors in Hataitai. I had told her we were from America, working in New Zealand for an evangelical missionary foundation, and wondered if she had any special requests that we could pray for with her. She shared that she was from Poland and her own children (who were about my age) were living in America. Before we left, she invited us to come again on Thursday for "tea." I thought she meant a cup of tea.

When we arrived, she seated us at a table in her living room with her husband, Rom, and four of her friends who had also emigrated from Poland to New Zealand shortly after World War II. Yania explained that she was celebrating her name day. "It's the day I was christened in my church. We celebrate it instead of our birthdays," she explained. "Please enjoy yourself."

Spread before us were salads and a huge platter of cold cuts, piled high with ham and Belgium salami. She had cucumbers from Israel, pickled herrings (a Dutch recipe), tomatoes, cheese, sauerkraut, beetroot, and breads. I ate everything but the beetroot and was relieved when Yania finally cleared the plates away from the table.

What I didn't realize was that the evening of celebrating Yania's name day had only just begun! She returned from the kitchen with a huge platter of Polish meatballs made from ground steak and marjoram seasoning, cooked inside homemade noodles. *Ah, the main course!* I thought. *I wouldn't have eaten seconds if I had known that more was coming.*

As we ate the delicious pasta, we listened to Yania tell the story of her separation from Rom when he was sent to a concentration camp in Siberia. "I left Poland on the ship with seven hundred children and one hundred adults," recalled my hostess as she passed the plate of beetroot one more time. "Most of the adults were sick, and the children were mischievous and uncontrollable. I didn't know if I would ever see Rom again, and I had no way of letting him know that I was headed for New Zealand."

Yania explained that her friends at the table had either been on the same ship with her or in the concentration camp with Rom. Everyone agreed that they loved American and New Zealand soldiers for helping them find freedom.

It was nearly seven o'clock when Yania stood to gather plates, again refusing help from any of us. Then to my utter surprise she returned from the kitchen with platters of chicken and roasted potatoes, peas, and marinated mushrooms with onions! I had never seen so much food come out of such a tiny kitchen.

Soon the conversation turned to happier memories of Poland before the war. Yania's friend, Jatiana, sat quietly through most of the stories, but occasionally her friends tried to pull her into the conversation, telling us how beautiful she was when she was young. She smiled modestly. "And we were all wealthy then," they said as they laughed and passed the roasted potatoes around the table. I couldn't imagine how wealth could improve the night we were sharing.

As the evening progressed and food was consumed, their gestures became exaggerated over their lively debates, and laughter flowed like running water. Eventually, Stan didn't bother to interpret for us because, even though we couldn't understand what they were saying, their expressive antics caught us up in the same laughter they all enjoyed. At about ten o'clock Yania brought coffee, small cakes, and doughnuts to finish the memorable celebration.

Yania showed me what the Lord may have meant when He said, "Here I am! I stand at the door and knock. If anyone hears my voice and opens the door, I will come in and eat with him, and he with me" (Revelation 3:20 NIV). Just as I knocked on Yania's door and was invited in to enjoy a most incredible meal, Jesus knocks on the door of our hearts, hoping to be invited in to share the daily celebration of our lives.

❧

When my publisher asked me to compile this book, I laughed because cooking isn't one of my natural talents, but I have learned that it can be an acquired skill. Perhaps I was intimidated from my earlier attempts to impress my soon-to-be husband. The first time I invited Jim to lunch after church, I realized I had locked myself out of my apartment. I called the fire department explaining my situation: "I left the gas oven on to bake a ham while I was away, and now I'm locked out of the house. Do you think there is danger of fire? Could you help me get into my house?" I begged. It must have been a slow day at the fire department, because within minutes their sirens were heard racing to my neighborhood.

Jim took a walk around the block, pretending not to know me, while brave firemen climbed their ladders to my second-story window and rescued my first attempt at a burnt offering. The ham was perfect in spite of the sirens and drama. But I have burned many meals since that day, so now Jim comes to the kitchen as soon as he hears the rattle of cooking utensils. He keeps our meals from burning while I look for something to use as a centerpiece on the table—candles make everything look better.

And we have great memories from the days that we do cook. Home-cooked meals continue to lure our grown children and grandchildren to the table to spend a few moments of their day with us. We ask them what they have learned lately, and sometimes we take turns proclaiming what we like about each person at the table. There is an old saying that "the family that prays together stays together." I'd add that the family who eats together will come home for the holidays.

When I announced my pursuit of stories for this work, I asked people to write about times they were aware of God's presence while enjoying His provision of daily bread. I haven't tested all of the recipes, so we must beg a disclaimer if your meal doesn't turn out quite right. But we do guarantee that if you invite the Lord to your meal, giving thanks for His provision, asking Him to bless what has been prepared by the work of your hands, you will always have enough for everyone at the table, and soon you will be able to fill your own journal with lessons you learn from God while cooking.

# Breakfast and Breads

# Starting with an Egg

**by Ada Nicholson Brownell**

*For you created my inmost being; you knit me together in my mother's womb. I praise you because I am fearfully and wonderfully made.*
PSALM 139:13–14 NIV

What do you see when you look at a raw egg in a bowl? Breakfast? Yummy desserts?

Or do you wonder what kind of chicken would have hatched had it been fertilized and kept at the right temperature? A hen? A rooster? Red? White? Brown? Do you see the spindly legs? Do you see the comb? Hear the hen's cluck or the rooster's crow?

A hen requires twenty-four to twenty-six hours to produce an egg. Thirty minutes later she starts all over, according to the American Egg Board. Hens with white feathers and earlobes produce white-shelled eggs. Hens with red feathers and red earlobes produce brown-shelled eggs. There is no nutritional difference between brown- and white-shelled eggs, or between fertilized and unfertilized eggs.

Eggs are high in nutrients, particularly protein and vitamins. Cloudiness of raw eggs occurs in some fresh eggs because carbon dioxide hasn't had time to escape through the shell. A slight yellow or greenish cast in the raw white may indicate riboflavin, one of the B vitamins. The harmless greenish ring in hard-cooked eggs is due to iron and sulfur compounds formed after overcooking or not cooling quickly. The stringy white pieces in the white are chalazae, which is edible and keeps the yolk in the center.

There's a lot to know about eggs, and God knows everything about us. I stared at an egg recently and recalled that we started as eggs—about the size of a sugar grain. Even then, God loved us and had a plan for our lives. God told Jeremiah, "Before I formed you in the womb I knew you, before you were born I set you apart" (Jeremiah 1:5 NIV).

He loved us when we were conceived; through the first cell division; and at twenty days when the foundations of our brains, spinal cords, and nervous systems were laid; at twenty-four days when our hearts began to beat; and continuously as we grew in our mother's womb. When God looked at Jeremiah, He saw a prophet; God sees someone special when He looks at each of us, too.

*Heavenly Father, thank You for the miraculous body in which I live, designed by You and loved by You. Help me to fulfill Your will for my life.*

## Breakfast Crustless Quiche
Preheat oven 350° F.
Cookware needed: small saucepan,
9 x 13 x 2-inch baking dish

Ingredients:
1/4 pound butter
1/2 cup flour
6 large eggs
1 cup milk
2 cups cottage cheese
1 pound Monterey Jack cheese, cubed
1 (3-ounce) package cream cheese, softened
1/2 teaspoon baking powder
1/2 teaspoon salt
1 teaspoon sugar

Directions: Melt butter in small saucepan; add flour and cook until smooth; set aside to let cool slightly. Beat eggs; add milk, cheeses, baking powder, salt, sugar, and butter-flour mixture. Stir until well blended. Pour into well-greased baking pan. Bake uncovered for 45 minutes. May add mushrooms, bacon, etc. Serves 8.

Cooking Tip: Return eggs to refrigerator as quickly as possible. When a recipe calls for eggs to be at room temperature, remove eggs from the refrigerator about 20 to 30 minutes before you need them, or put them in a bowl of warm water while you assemble other ingredients. Eggs age quicker in one day at room temperature than a week refrigerated. Fresh eggs keep 4 to 5 weeks refrigerated in their carton.

**Ada Brownell**, the youngest of eight siblings, spent her early years in the kitchen washing dishes. Marriage, five children, and six grandchildren got her out of the sink and to the mixing bowl. She finds cooking a pleasure and sometimes surprising. She is a retired newspaper reporter and has written for Christian publications for more than forty years.

# Taste and See

**by Sandra McVicker-Dalrymple**

*So God created man in his own image,*
*in the image of God created he him;*
*male and female created he them.*
GENESIS 1:27 KJV

I'm an artist. Eating isn't an option, so it is clear why I see cooking and food preparation as an art form. I know I am *destined* to eat that next meal (and the next), so I continually seek delightful new recipes. Finding a good recipe is like finding an inspirational treasure.

A good recipe for me has three components: It tastes great, is simple to prepare, and hopefully is a visual delight. I find all the colors and textures of the different ingredients to be exciting.

Once or twice a year, I open my art studio and invite friends to see my work, taste my new recipes, and share the simplicity of our friendship. The day of celebration holds the same components of success as my favorite recipes: great tastes, simple preparation, and visual delights.

In both my art and cooking, I've learned to never be intimidated by someone else's ability. Watching a confident trained chef can cause knees to quake, hands to tremble, and brains to scramble, but this is why all TV cooking programs should be viewed as entertainment.

I may enjoy the gifted performance of a symphony or an opera, but this perfection can't stifle the rousing songs from my own heart or enthusiastic hums of my favorite tunes as I follow my Father's footsteps and create what is in my heart to express.

I adore pancakes, so I searched for the perfect sur-garless pancake recipe, but I never found it. One day I said, "I'll make it up myself!" And I did. I often find that God has hidden His answers within my own creativity. Paul wrote, "I can do everything through him who gives me strength" (Philippians 4:13 NIV).

The most essential ingredient for any recipe is love. Be generous with the love, follow the recipe, and use good ingredients. And storing God's Word in our hearts is also essential for success—His direction never misses the mark. As we bravely follow His instructions and include the right ingredients, we know a good outcome is assured—a palate not disappointed and simple effort rewarded by praise.

*Father, I pray that our hands enjoy the
creativity You give us. May we know there are
no limits with You. You are our purpose, and
Your love is the compass to enjoy the ordinary.
Thank You for guiding us and giving us the
skill to do all things without fear or regret.*

## Lovely Pancakes

Cookware needed: stovetop skillet (preferably iron)

Ingredients:
1/4 level teaspoon kosher salt
1 level teaspoon baking powder
1 cup loose (not packed down) unbleached
    all-purpose flour (no chemicals added)
1 large brown egg (tastes better)
2 tablespoons cooking oil
2 generous tablespoons plain (genuine) yogurt
2 level tablespoons sour cream (optional)*
Half-and-half or soy milk

*The sour cream can be eliminated by using more
half-and-half. For a *super-duper* variation: Use the liquid from a can of apricots in place of the sour cream,
and serve the drained apricots with the pancakes.

Directions: Mix salt, baking powder, and flour.
In a one-cup measuring cup add egg, oil, yogurt, and
sour cream, then fill the remainder of the cup with

half-and-half. Transfer to a separate mixing bowl and blend together well before adding to the dry ingredients. Add dry mixture to the wet ingredients and stir thoroughly. Heat skillet to a medium temperature. Test a small pancake (grease skillet with oil or butter, if needed). Flip cake over when a bubble appears (or if you get nervous). Serve with butter, honey, jam, or maple syrup.

Cooking Tip: Always crack an egg into a separate cup before adding it to batter. Use a serrated grapefruit spoon to remove any eggshells that fall into the cup with the egg.

**Sandra McVicker-Dalrymple** is an illustrator, writer, and compulsive cartoonist. She studied painting and photography at the San Francisco Art Institute (aka California School of Fine Arts). She fell in love with words and color, which birthed her quest for meaningful expression in a world of books and art—a compactable mix that brings fulfillment and delights her heart.

# Culinary Cure

**by Niki Anderson**

*When he was at the table with them,*
*he took bread, gave thanks,*
*broke it and began to give it to them.*
*Then their eyes were opened and they recognized him.*
LUKE 24:30–31 NIV

With the help of a fistful of dough, God has nursed me through various stages of spiritual, emotional, and physical healing. My kitchen doubles as household galley and rehabilitation center. Only in the last few years did I discover my kitchen cure-all.

By nature I'm cheery. A difficult day or a discouraging week may leave me downcast on occasion. More often, I'm even-tempered and joyful. But a series of events including the death of our grandchild, unrelenting pain from a bulging disk, and a succession of back-to-back deadlines plunged me into a season of depression. During my recovery

I discovered a free, self-help therapy—baking.

After His resurrection, Jesus appeared to two people on the road to Emmaus. Failing to recognize Him, they conversed about His innocence and His crucifixion in Jerusalem. Hours later as Christ and His wayside travelers lingered over a meal, scripture says, "Jesus was recognized by them when he broke the bread" (Luke 24:35 NIV). Jesus described Himself as the Bread of Life. He chose bread to symbolize His body and included it in the Communion meal He established in His memory.

Could it be that in the process of preparing food that we memorialize the Savior who is sustenance and healing for the world? Perhaps in the kneading of a loaf, the mixing of a cake, or the assembling of nutrients we commune with Jesus, the true Bread of Life.

Though I am well past those months of depression, I still usher myself to the kitchen, select a new and intriguing recipe, and bake for therapy. Different from my son who deals with stress by heading with his snowboard to a mountaintop or my husband who hits the pavement on his Harley-Davidson, I blend ingredients, shape a cookie ball, or whip a batter to relieve tension, to relax after a long day, or to ease my heart when life weighs heavily.

What have I learned from God while cooking? Healing happens when I'm near the Bread of Life. Try baking and be healed!

*Dear Lord, nurture me as I prepare food
with You—the staple of life.*

## Niki's Favorite Scones
Modification of "Shepherds' World-Famous Scones"
(Did you know the proper British
pronunciation is *scawns*?)

Preheat oven to 350° F.
Cookware needed: baking sheet

Ingredients:
3 cups self-rising flour*
1/2 cup sugar
1/2 cup (1 stick) cold unsalted butter, cut into bits
6 ounces (about 1 1/2 cups) dried fruit (I use diced
   dried apricots, chopped dates, or Craisins)
1/2 to 1 cup chopped walnuts or pecans
4 ounces (1/2 cup) buttermilk
4 ounces (1/2 cup) light whipping cream

*If you do not have self-rising flour, add 1 table-
spoon baking powder and 1/2 teaspoon salt to flour
mixture.

Glacé Ingredients:
1/2 cup powdered sugar
1/4 teaspoon vanilla
1 tablespoon milk or cream

Directions: Sift the flour and sugar into a bowl and add the butter. Blend the mixture until it resembles coarse cornmeal. Stir in the dried fruit and nuts. Add the buttermilk and cream, a little at a time, and blend the mixture until it forms a soft—but not sticky—dough. On a lightly floured surface, form the dough into a round ball about 1 inch thick (measure height). With a 2-inch cookie cutter, (or 2-inch diameter glass rim) cut out the rounds. Transfer the rounds to a buttered baking sheet and bake for 10 to 20 minutes or until lightly golden and until bottoms sound hollow when tapped. Don't overcook! Yield: about 11 scones.

Glacé: Mix powdered sugar, vanilla, and milk or cream. Brush over cooled scones.

Cooking Tip: Keep a plastic ruler in your utensil drawer. Use it for measuring piecrust and dough ball diameters. When the breadboard work is complete, use the ruler's clean edge to scrap the remaining flour into the wastebasket.

---

**Niki Anderson** is the author of national best-seller *What My Cat Has Taught Me about Life*, and its sequel, *Ins-pur-r-rational Stories for Cat Lovers*, and writer of the premier release of *What I Learned from God While Gardening*.

# Doughnut Holes

**by Ruth McHaney Danner**

*You have set our iniquities before You,*
*our secret sins in the light of Your countenance.*
PSALM 90:8 NKJV

"**M**mm, this is really good!" My pastor's wife, a meticulous veteran cook, finally had a reason to compliment my efforts. She'd just taken a bite of one of my homemade doughnut holes at the church potluck. As a new bride, I beamed while she praised my attempt at something besides macaroni and cheese from a box.

"And they're crème-filled, too!" she continued, finishing that donut hole and starting another.

*What?* My mind raced. *Crème-filled?* I hadn't made crème-filled doughnuts.

Not wanting to spoil the moment, I recovered from the shock of her words and tasted one for myself. Sure enough, it was gooey on the inside.

Gooey—not *crème*-filled.

I mentally reviewed my cooking process:

*Mix the dough, then heat the oil to the correct temperature, using a candy thermometer*—check.

*Drop the dough by spoon-sized balls into the hot oil, cooking the balls three minutes*—check.

*Remove the doughnut balls and drain on paper towels, then roll in powdered sugar*—check, check, check. I'd done it all. What could've happened?

Meanwhile, Pastor's wife had started on doughnut number three. "Why, this one's *not* crème-filled! Did you do something different here?"

I looked at the doughnut half she was holding. It was small—smaller than many of the others. That's when I realized my error: All the spoonfuls of dough hadn't been the same size. The smaller ones had cooked completely, while the larger ones were still raw in the middle when I pulled them out after the allotted time.

So that explained it. But the more pressing problem was how to confess to this scrupulous cook that she'd just consumed two lumps of raw doughnut. Upon hearing the news, she would gag and run to the restroom. Others who'd eaten the doughnuts would follow. I envisioned a near-riot, complete with flashing ambulance lights and news cameras. Even worse, I would be branded as a culinary menace, forever sentenced to bringing mac and cheese mixes to future potlucks.

So I cleared my throat. "Well," I said, answering her question carefully, "I just followed the recipe—with a few simple variations."

*Father, no matter how successful we are at deceiving others, nothing is hid from You. Help us to recognize our faults, confess them, and find forgiveness from those whom we transgress against, and also forgive others because Your mercy is great to love and forgive us.*

### Filled Doughnuts

Cookware needed: deep fryer or
deep stovetop saucepan

Ingredients:
1 cup lukewarm milk
1/3 cup sugar
1 teaspoon salt
1 package active dry yeast
2 cups flour, sifted
2 eggs, beaten
1/3 cup soft shortening
Up to 2 additional cups flour (mix into batter until stiff)
Canola oil for deep frying

Directions: Mix together milk, sugar, and salt. Mix together yeast and flour, then add to milk mixture, beating with electric mixer at medium-high speed. Mix together eggs and shortening, then add to previous mixture. Gradually add about 2 more cups of flour, mixing with spoon or by hand, until dough is stiff enough to knead. Knead until smooth, about 8 minutes, adding more flour to prevent stickiness. Place in a greased bowl and let dough rise until double, about one hour. Punch dough down, then divide in half. Roll out each half to about 3/8-inch thickness. Cut into squares (using a knife) or rounds (using a cookie cutter). Place a teaspoonful of jelly on half of the pieces. Using the others, cover the jellied halves and crimp the edges to seal them. Let them rise about 30 minutes more, then fry a few at a time in canola oil at 375 degrees for 1 minute each. Drain on paper towels and roll in sugar. Makes about 2 dozen filled doughnut holes.

Cooking Tip: Use a cook's scale to weigh dough before dropping it into the oil. The extra effort allows each of your spoonfuls to be the same size. Try this when making muffins, cookies, or any other individual items. A uniform size will ensure uniform cooking.

**Ruth McHaney Danner** is a writer from Spokane, Washington. She's also a professional quilter, and her book, *What I Learned from God While Quilting*, is available from Barbour Publishing.

# Pray and Bake

**by Louise Tucker Jones**

*Pray without ceasing.*
1 THESSALONIANS 5:17 KJV

I answered the phone to hear my husband's panicked voice. "I've been in a car wreck!"

Adrenaline hit me. "Where are you? Are you okay?"

"My back is hurting."

I was terrified and wanted to go to the accident site, but Carl advised against it because of the bad weather. He assured me that an ambulance was on the way, and he would call later.

I immediately started praying. "Lord, please let Carl be okay. Please!" I walked the floor for a while, then jerked a bowl of muffin batter from the refrigerator and preheated the oven. Time to bake! My mind and heart could pray while my hands stayed busy. With hardly a thought, I placed cupcake liners in the muffin pan and threw some chocolate chips into the batter, something I had never done with this particular recipe. I stirred in the chocolate morsels, poured the dough into the muffin tin, and popped it into the oven, praying all the while.

Baking always presented an escape from my worry and helped me "pray without ceasing." When my oldest son called home from Japan, he had no idea that his favorite pastries were sitting on the kitchen cabinet since I had "prayed and baked" during his long flight.

The phone rang again. The paramedics assessed Carl's injuries—nothing critical. When he got home, I took him to the emergency room where a doctor determined his back injury to be muscular in nature. The seat belt kept Carl safe but also wrenched his back upon impact. However, that could be solved with medication and rest at home.

Later that evening, I curled up in the recliner and relaxed with a muffin, a cup of hot tea, and a thankful heart. It had been an emotional day, but God graciously answered my prayer for Carl's safety. Snuggling into the chair, I bit into the muffin. The chocolate chips that I had thrown into the batter soothed my taste buds. *Hmm, this is good. I'll have to do this again—without an emergency!*

*Thank You, Lord, that I can pray to You anyplace and anytime. Thank You for protecting my family and giving me "work" to do with my hands while my heart and mind are in Your presence.*

## Raisin Bran Muffins

Preheat oven to 400° F.
Cookware needed: muffin tins

Ingredients:
5 cups flour
1 1/2 cups sugar (may use part honey)
3 teaspoons baking soda
1/2 teaspoon salt
1 cup oil
4 eggs
1 quart buttermilk
1 (15-ounce) box Raisin Bran*

*For extra-moist muffins, use less than the full box of cereal and crunch the flakes somewhat with a rolling pin so they aren't so large. Also allow batter to sit in refrigerator for a day before baking; this allows for the cereal to soak up the liquid.

Directions: Mix flour, sugar, baking soda, and salt in large bowl. Mix oil, eggs, and buttermilk in separate bowl and beat well. Add liquid mixture to dry ingredients and beat well. Add bran flakes (and nuts if desired). Optional: Add nuts, chocolate chips, etc. (I add them only to the amount of muffins that

I am baking at a given time.) Pour into greased or paper-lined muffin tins. Bake for 15 to 20 minutes. Store batter in tightly covered container—this will keep 4 to 6 weeks in the refrigerator. Makes about 4 dozen muffins.

Cooking Tip: Dipping fresh fruit, such as apples and bananas, in 7UP will not only keep them from turning brown, but will also aid them in retaining their natural flavor.

**Louise Tucker Jones** is an award-winning author and inspi-rational speaker. Her books include *Dance from the Heart* and *Extraordinary Kids* (coauthored), along with contributions to over a dozen compilation books and numerous magazines, including *Guideposts* and *Angels on Earth*. Louise resides in Edmond, Oklahoma.

# My Lover's Gift— Was He Serious?

**by Jan Tickner**

*They that wait upon the LORD shall renew their
strength; they shall mount up with wings as eagles;
they shall run, and not be weary;
and they shall walk, and not faint.*
ISAIAH 40:31 KJV

Another package from that boyfriend of yours,
but this time I think he's sent a brick." My postman,
laughing, handed me the bulky package. I giggled.

It was 1943, I was sixteen, in love, and my handsome air force lieutenant, Russell Tickner, had left
for overseas combat. He counted on these little no-
occasion gifts to help bridge distance and time. What
neither of us knew were the many miles and months
they would ultimately span—months he spent missing in action.

Layers of wrapping paper later and. . .finally! There it was! *The Woman's Home Companion Cook Book.* *Cookbook?* I was stunned. Inscribed on the flyleaf were these words: "Darling, if you learn all these recipes, I'll never complain. So go to work. Love, Russell."

On a following page, I read a Wartime Postscript: "In a fine spirit of patriotism American homemakers have adapted themselves to. . .changes. . . Minds are open to new ideas. . . Though you may have to wait until the war is over to try some. . ." Giggles turned to tears. *Wait? How long, Lord?*

It seemed like forever waiting for Russ's return. Waiting for our wedding. We looked forward to a family—ultimately, four healthy, hungry children. From that point it was the needed patience for cookies to bake or bread to rise.

Today the threadbare cookbook stands tall among other less significant recipe volumes. With every stained page turned, with every new recipe tried, or every old dish revisited, I'm reminded of God's lesson that I believe began that day; it was not an easy one. In time God led me to discover the joy of cooking, while experiencing the related pressure and ultimate pleasure of patience.

Now a widow, "Gran," and "Great-Gran," God continues ministering the spiritual and culinary significance of "waiting."

*Thank You, Father God, for Your Word
and the lesson of patience. How many
times I have relied on Your promise of
much-needed renewed strength.*

## Fruit Torte

The aforementioned "Wartime Postscript" included
mention of those recipes that would "add interest and
novelty" to our wartime menus, such as a Fruit
Torte—that is, if you had extra sugar rations.

Preheat oven to 350° F.
Cookware needed: 9 x 11-inch baking pan

Ingredients:
1 cup flour
1 teaspoon cinnamon
1/2 teaspoon salt
1 1/2 teaspoons baking powder
1/2 cup butter
1/2 cup sugar
2 eggs, well beaten
1 tablespoon lemon juice
1/2 teaspoon grated lemon rind

Topping ingredients:
Fruit (see options)*
1 teaspoon cinnamon
1/2 cup sugar

*Options: Ten plums, equivalent number of slices of tart apple, or dried apricots (soaked and cooked without sugar and well drained).

Directions: Sift flour; add cinnamon, salt, and baking powder. Sift all again. Cream butter; gradually add sugar and cream together until light and fluffy. Add well-beaten eggs and beat until creamy. Add lemon juice and rind. Stir flour mixture into creamed mixture, sifting about 1/4 cup at a time. Pour into a greased pan. Press fruit into batter and sift cinnamon and sugar over top. (Or pour half of the batter into pan; spread a layer of fruit; sprinkle with sugar and cinnamon; pour remaining batter on top and bake.) Bake about 1 hour.

Cooking Tip: Before whipping cream, chill the bowl and beaters in the freezer. To 1 cup of whipping cream, add 1 tablespoon of granulated sugar and 1 teaspoon vanilla. Mix slowly for 30 seconds to blend well, then beat on high until volume doubles. Great in coffee, too!

Note: Wartime Postscript—*Woman's Home Companion Cook Book*, published 1942, 1943, 1944 by P. F. Collier & Son Corporation, page 28.

**Jan Tickner** is an author, Amy Foundation award-winner, and freelance journalist who wears many hats. She is a teacher, writer, author, public speaker, and magazine contributor. A widow, she is—in her *spare time*—mother of four, grandmother of nine, and great-grandmother of six.

# Hot Out of the Oven

**by Linda LaMar Jewell**

*Go thy way, eat thy bread with joy.*
ECCLESIASTES 9:7 KJV

Sighing with approval, I sampled the fresh, home-made Ethiopian honey bread another mother, Linda Strascina, brought to our first-graders' tasting party.

After complimenting Linda, I described my bread-making disaster. The lonely loaf I attempted as a newlywed resembled a cinder block: hard, heavy, gray, and inedible. When I threw away my culinary calamity, I also threw in the proverbial bread-baking towel.

When I finished telling my story, Linda chuckled, then said, "Oh, it's easy when you know how. Proof the yeast by following the package directions. Use a candy thermometer to test the water temperature. Oh, and don't put in too much flour or the dough will be heavy. And knead it, knead it, knead it." Linda demonstrated the kneading action with her graceful, expressive hands.

Our conversation encouraged me to try again. Following Linda's simple instructions, God erased my self-addressed label, "bread-making failure," when I had the success she described. In fact, now one of my signature kitchen specialties is homemade bread.

I take delight in baking bread. I ponder analogies about God's creativity while enthusiastically stirring flour into small clouds up to my elbows. I enjoy the rhythm of kneading dough. God also shows me the satisfaction of achieving tangible results when a sticky lump of humdrum ingredients like flour, water, eggs, milk, shortening, yeast, sugar, and salt transforms into a smooth, elastic mound of bread dough.

Twenty-five years ago, Linda could never have foreseen how her practical advice and encouragement would continue to bless my family. I got back into the kitchen where God taught me that when I'm baking bread I'm also making warm family memories. Now we linger in the kitchen anticipating hot rolls fresh from the oven.

The scent of warm baking bread rekindles my childhood memories. I reminisce about my grandparents, sisters, and me gathering around the kitchen table, sampling fresh homemade bread and butter— and I smile. Thanks to God's grace through Linda, I learned it took only some practical advice and a few words of encouragement to change self-talk from "I can't" to "I can."

*Lord, help us to do good unto others as*
*others have done good unto us. Instead*
*of hoarding our knowledge, give us Your*
*grace to share practical tips to equip and*
*encourage young cooks to get back in the kitchen*
*and make warm family memories.*

## Refrigerator Rolls

This is one of my favorite hot roll recipes from Great-Aunt Ora Frame in my family cookbook, *In-laws and Outlaws and Two Kinds of Cheeses: The Frame Family Cookbook.* To make warm memories, when the rolls are almost done, call your family members to the kitchen for piping hot bread right out of the oven. Serve with your family's favorite jam, jelly, honey, or butter—along with family stories.

Preheat oven to 400° F.
Cookware needed: cookie sheets

Ingredients:
1 cup milk
1/2 cup sugar
1 1/2 teaspoons salt
1 cup boiling water
1/2 cup shortening
2 (1/4-ounce) packages active dry yeast
1/4 cup lukewarm water

Pinch of sugar
2 eggs, beaten
6 1/2 cups bread flour

Directions: Scald milk (on stovetop or in micro-wave); heat just until milk begins to form tiny bubbles around the edge of the pan or cup. Add sugar and salt. Stir and set aside.

To boiling water, add shortening; set aside and let shortening melt. Proof yeast in lukewarm water with a pinch of sugar. After yeast proofs, combine all previous ingredients in a large crockery bread bowl.

Stir in eggs, then add bread flour. Stir with a fork or large wooden spoon. Knead dough. Dough will be very sticky, so remove rings, bracelets, and watch. Rub hands with flour and knead dough until it is no longer sticky. Resist the urge to add more flour. Continue to knead the dough for about 10 to 12 minutes. Although the dough may still be a little tacky, it will become more smooth and elastic.

Leave dough in a large bowl, because it needs room to rise. Cover bowl tightly with plastic wrap and refrigerate dough for at least 1 hour. The dough may be stored in the refrigerator for as long as three days.

To make rolls, remove the dough from the refrigerator and let it stand (approximately 1 to 3 hours in a warm (about 85° F) area until dough is pliable enough to work. Lightly grease two cookie sheets with shortening. Punch dough down and form it into rolls.

Place rolls on cookie sheets and cover loosely with clean tea towels. Place cookie sheets with rolls in a warm area until rolls are doubled in size (approximately 1 hour).

This recipe makes approximately 24 to 30 large rolls or about 70 to 80 bite-sized rolls. Bake rolls for 15 minutes for bite-sized rolls, or 20 minutes for large rolls, or until they are golden brown (both top and bottom) and sound hollow when you gently tap them.

Cooking Tip: Proofing yeast means "proving it is alive." Check the expiration date on the package to make sure the active dry yeast is fresh. With a candy thermometer, test warm water before adding active dry yeast. Water should be between 100° and 110° F. If the water is too cold or too hot, the yeast will not activate or will die—either way the dough will not rise. Add a pinch of sugar to warm water. Sprinkle active dry yeast on the top of the water and let it sit for about 10 minutes. If the yeast foams, it is alive. If it doesn't foam, the yeast is dead. If the yeast is dead, throw it away—don't add it to your other ingredients. Instead, go to the grocery store and buy fresh active dry yeast.

Through a writing and speaking ministry, **Linda LaMar Jewell** encourages you to seek answers in the Bible to your relationship questions. She also teaches note writing and journaling workshops.

# Home Sweet-Smelling Home

### by Marie Asner

*A measure of wheat for a penny, and three
measures of barley for a penny; and see thou hurt
not the oil and the wine.*
REVELATION 6:6 KJV

**M**y husband and I were newly married and transferred to jobs six hundred miles from our homes. In order to make our apartment feel *and smell* like home, I began to bake bread every weekend. The aroma of baking bread reminded me of Mom's kitchen and helped quell loneliness in a new place.

Unknown to me, each weekend the odor of baking bread also reached other tenants. I thought we had moved to quite a friendly four-plex as people were offering to open car doors for me, carry grocery bags, and walk our puppy. After a few weeks, I finally realized it was the smell of baking bread that piqued their interest, so we decided to invite neighbors for a meal and give them a loaf of bread to take back to their apartment.

The first guests were two army officers who shared an apartment while attending military school. They arrived for the Saturday evening meal well groomed and bearing a large bouquet of flowers. During the meal, the men ate enough bread for the entire platoon, and when I presented them with a loaf to take with them, the argument began—which one was to carry the loaf back to their apartment?

The next morning, as my husband and I went through the front door of the apartment building, we were greeted with the sight of one of the soldiers doing push-ups on the lawn. That morning, he had cut the loaf of bread in half and kept the larger half for himself—hence the "punishment" from his friend.

"Wars start like this," my husband murmured under his breath as I got the men another loaf.

We lived in that apartment complex for six more months until being transferred. I learned that loneliness is present everywhere, and the smell of "home" can be a comfort to everyone. I continued to bake bread every weekend and felt that God was using me to keep peace in our four-plex. The landlord even told us that was the happiest building he'd had in years.

*Lord, thank You for the many blessings*
*You bestow on us and the gifts You give us,*
*which we may share with others. A gift of*
*a meal, a gift of friendship, and a gift of peace*

*are among the things that You have given*
*us which we may give to others.*

## Soda Pop Bread
Preheat oven to 375° F.
Cookware needed: loaf pan

Ingredients:
1 1/2 cups ginger ale
2 tablespoons sugar
3 cups self-rising flour

Directions: Mix the ingredients slowly and care-fully until well mixed. Pour into a well-greased pan. Bake for 45 minutes. Good with honey butter or apple butter.

Cooking Tip: Lids from yogurt or margarine containers can be used as daily, disposable spoon holders when cooking. No need to purchase something extra for your kitchen counter. The lids can be used and tossed away after each meal preparation, or have your family wash and save them in a special container for this use.

# When Life Doesn't Gel

**by Lynne Cooper Sitton**

*No discipline seems pleasant at the time, but painful.
Later on, however, it produces a harvest of
righteousness and peace for those who have
been trained by it.*

HEBREWS 12:11 NIV

Steam, sweat, and tears mingled on my cheeks as I added sugar to a boiling pot of elderberry juice on my kitchen stove. "Lord," I prayed, "life seems like this hot bubbly mess. How could my parents criticize my new commitment to Christ?" Their accusation "You're so heavenly-minded, you're no earthly good!" stung. My heart burned with pain and anger. My mind simmered with righteous indignation, judgments, and clever retorts.

I stirred the mountain of sugar into the juice, quieting the bloodred mixture for a few seconds, before it rumbled to a splattering frenzy. Adding pectin, I stirred furiously and watched the pot erupt again. Wildly bubbling froth climbed the pot sides like a caged animal, ready to consume my hand!

"Just like this difficulty in my life," I mused, knowing the fiery torture must continue for *exactly* one minute to produce jelly. My spoon swirled frantically.

I counted the seconds: "Fifty-eight. . .alligator. . .fifty-nine. . .alligator. . .sixty!" Phew! Burner off! Armed with potholders, I moved the heavy pot of scalding liquid close to my sterilized jars. Immediately a skin coated the juice's surface as it cooled. I had to work fast. With another sterilized metal spoon, I began the purifying process, skimming off impurities hidden in the foam. Before pouring the jelly into jars, I had to stir and skim. . .stir and skim.

Each time I disturbed the hot liquid, little bubbles and specks rose to the surface for removal. They clung to the sides of the metal pot and my spoon. Finally the dark red elderberry juice glistened clear.

As I prepared to pour the thickening substance into containers, the Holy Spirit's soft voice nudged me. "I remove *your* impurities by 'stirring and skimming,' too! You need to release all those bubbles of hurt, disappointment, and anger to Jesus! I use perfect timing, temperature, and turmoil in your life to help you become clean and molded like your elderberry jelly. Let go, so I can give you peace!"

*Heavenly Father, I know You use difficulties
in my life to purify me. Thank You for guiding
and disciplining me. Thank You for stirring
me up and removing the impurities I can't see,
so that I may live a righteous life. Please
mold me into the image of Your Son.*

## Elderberry Jelly

(Use exact measurements, ripe fruit, and
commercial pectin with instructions for
jelly making. Do not double recipe.)

Pick fruit: Elderberry bushes grow wild in most
climates along roads and highways, in meadows or
median strips. Identify them by the wide, flat clus-
ters of white blossoms, which turn into small black-
ish berries. Elderberries are used in making wine, pie
filling, and jelly, but are difficult to find in stores.

Prepare juice: For each batch of jelly, wash 3
pounds of fruit, removing large stems. In a large
saucepan, crush berries by thin layers and heat until
juice starts to bubble. Simmer covered for 15 minutes,
stirring occasionally. Place fruit/juice in a jelly bag to
collect juice in a large container. For very clear jelly, allow fruit juice to drip undisturbed into the container.
Gently squeeze the bag if you don't care about perfect
clarity. Juice extraction can take several hours or overnight. Refrigerate or freeze juice until ready to use.

Prepare containers: Wash 8-ounce jelly jars and sterilize them in boiling water for 10 minutes. Keep jars upside down in hot water until filling. Place jar caps or new canning lids and screw tops into boiling water just before filling jars. Lift lids and jars with sterilized tongs, not hands or potholders. If sealing jars with paraffin, melt it in an old double boiler or aluminum container in hot water so you can easily ladle or pour it. Place newspaper or paper towels on the countertop for easy cleanup, and arrange hot jars for easy pouring access just before filling.

Follow manufacturer's directions: Commercial pectin like Certo and Sure-Jell provide recipes and directions for jelly making. Each product gives exact quantities and measurements.

Cooking Tip: Keep a small saucepan of boiling water and clean paper towels handy while you fill jelly jars. If you dribble jelly on the rim, inside, or threads of a jar, dip the corner of a paper towel into the sterile water and wipe away the drip. Your jar stays sterile for paraffin or vacuum lid sealing.

**Lynne Cooper Sitton**, a published writer and illustrator living in Coral Springs, Florida, with her husband, serves as president of the Broward County Chapter of the American Christian Writers Association. A recent breast cancer survivor, she is mother of two grown sons and "Nana" to a beautiful granddaughter.

# Soups and Side Dishes

# While Brewing Tea

**by Maxine Holmgren**

*Let them give thanks to the LORD for his unfailing love
and his wonderful deeds for men, for he satisfies the
thirsty and fills the hungry with good things.*
PSALM 107:8–9 NIV

Every time I brew a cup of tea, I think of what
Eleanor Roosevelt said: "Women are like tea bags. Put
them in hot water and their true strength emerges."

When the tea bag is sitting on the shelf in its
colorful box, carefully wrapped in a protective shield,
it stays nice and fresh. We're like that, too. When
we're wrapped up in our peaceful lifestyle and everything is going well, we feel nice and secure.

Like individuals, every tea has a different
personality. There are also different grades of teas,
from premium to low-grade, just as there are
different levels of faith. Like people, some teas are
strong and full of flavor, and some are very aromatic,

but without much substance. There are teas known for their calming, soothing effect and teas that give strength and energy. Some of the weaker teas are tasteless and just grow lukewarm as they steep.

But what happens when we are yanked out of our comfort zone? Like a tea bag that is unwrapped and plunked into a cup of hot water, we can find ourselves plunked into a cup of trouble. Now the real test begins. What will emerge as the hot water uncurls the little dried tea leaves? What level of strength emerges from us as we are steeped in difficulty?

Just as a tea bag hangs from a string tag, we, too, have a lifeline to which we can hold: Jesus. As we hold on to Him, we feel His peace emerge, and He flavors our troubled waters. His power and energy moves through our situations, changing our despair to hope through faith in His promises. And as we trust Jesus, He becomes the flavorful strength that anchor our souls, and we become the tag that is lifted and draped securely outside the cup of hot water.

The lift we get from a cup of tea lasts only a short time, but the lift we get from Jesus is long lasting. In fact, it will take us all the way to heaven.

*Father in heaven, I praise You and thank You that You have created each one of us in a different way. You have given us different strengths, different talents, and different gifts. I thank You that to all of us, You have offered*

*the wonderful gifts of Your love and peace. You*
*fill our cup with whatever is needed*
*to make our lives complete. Help us, dear Lord,*
*to grow stronger in You every day.*

## Chamomile Tea Cauliflower Soup
From *Cooking with Tea* by J. and M. Siegel

Cookware needed: large saucepan, small sauté pan

Ingredients:
6 chamomile tea bags
3 cups water
1 large head cauliflower, cut into small pieces
1/4 cup onion, chopped
2 stalks celery, chopped
1 tablespoon butter
Salt and pepper, to taste

Directions: Boil water; add tea bags for 5 minutes. Remove tea bags. Add cauliflower to the tea, cover and simmer for 15 minutes, or until tender. Drain, reserving 1 cup of the liquid. In a small pan, sauté onions and celery in butter. Put in a blender with the cauliflower mixture and the reserved cooking liquid. Blend until smooth and serve. Serves 4 to 6.

Cooking Tip: Bake potatoes in a muffin tin to easily remove them from a hot oven.

**Maxine Holmgren** is a freelance writer, speaker, and Bible study leader who loves tea parties. She belongs to a Victorian Tea Society and writes a column for their newsletter. She has written a mystery tea party game booklet that is sold on eBay and in tearooms. She is also active in the local community theater group and appears in stage plays. Maxine lives with her husband in Sun City, California.

# The Great Corn Bread Cook-off

**by Kitty Chappell**

*For where you have envy and selfish ambition,*
*there you find disorder and every evil practice.*
*But the wisdom that comes from heaven is first of*
*all pure; then peace-loving, considerate. . .full of*
*mercy and good fruit. . .and sincere.*
JAMES 3:16–17 NIV

Wolfing down a third helping of corn bread, my husband Jerry gushed to our hostess, "This corn bread is delicious!" To make matters worse, he turned to me and said, "Isn't Debbie's corn bread great?"

"Yes," I mumbled, my heart turning green.

Debbie beamed as she said, "Thank you."

Jerry used to rave about my corn bread until I got on my "health food kick." I'd been using nothing but "stone-ground whole wheat flour" in every thing, including corn bread. There was no way I could compete with Debbie's light, fluffy recipe.

*Maybe I should compromise.*

One afternoon over coffee, I swallowed my pride and asked Debbie for her recipe. (I had thrown mine out.)

"I'm sorry, you know I don't share my recipes. I don't understand why you give copies to everyone in the world. Don't you realize that when you do that, you don't have anything that's your 'specialty'?" she chided. I fumed all the way home.

"What's wrong, honey?" Jerry asked.

"Debbie refused to share her corn bread recipe," I complained. "I just want to make good corn bread for you," I stammered, tears flowing unexpectedly.

"You used to make great corn bread! You'll do it again."

We didn't have corn bread that often, only when I cooked pinto beans, but I was motivated! After several attempts, Jerry reported, "It's good, honey, but not quite there yet."

During my next attempt, I suddenly realized something—I cared more about competing with Debbie than I did in pleasing Jerry. "I'm sorry, Lord," I whispered.

That day Jerry exclaimed, "You've done it—this corn bread is every bit as good as Debbie's!"

Weeks later, during dinner at Debbie's, Jerry again praised her corn bread and gave me a sly wink. But this time, it didn't bother me.

Helping Debbie clean up, I opened the trash

compactor to discard something Debbie's corn bread secret—se of Jiffy Corn Muffin Mix. *I've bee mix?* I laughed inwardly and quickly

Debbie hadn't wanted to share secret, so the least I could do was help told no one—except Jerry.

*Dear Lord, please protect me from the temptation to compete with others. Motivate me to want to do my best so that You will be honored. And help me to realize that the most powerful tool in Your hand is a pure motive.*

### Taco Soup

Delicious with a thick slice of corn bread!

Cookware needed: large stovetop pan or Dutch oven

Ingredients:
1 pound ground hamburger or turkey
1/4 cup chopped onion
1 (16-ounce) can tomatoes
1 (14–16 ounce) can kidney beans and juice
1 (14–16 ounce) can whole kernel corn and juice
1 (14–16 ounce) can green beans and juice
1 (8-ounce) can tomato sauce
1 small can diced green chilies and juice
1 packet taco seasoning
On the side: shredded cheddar cheese and chips

tions: Sauté meat and onion until light
n. Add all other ingredients, except chips and
cheese. Bring to boil. Simmer covered 15 minutes.
Sprinkle individual servings with cheese and chips.
Serves 4–5 hearty eaters.

Cooking Tip: Go to your nearest grocer, purchase Jiffy Corn Muffin Mix, and follow directions.
After making corn bread from scratch that equaled
Jiffy's in taste and texture, I decided it was easier and
less time-consuming to just buy their mix. (When
I receive compliments, however, I always give the
credit to Jiffy.)

**Kitty Chappell** is a speaker and freelance writer. Her full-
length book, *Sins of a Father: Forgiving the Unforgivable*, was
recently released by New Hope Publishers. Kitty and her
husband, Jerry, live near Phoenix, Arizona.

# Labors of Love

## by Jamie Meredith

*Beloved, let us love one another: for love is of God;*
*and every one that loveth is born of God,*
*and knoweth God.*
1 JOHN 4:7 KJV

It is easy to forget the importance of little things and what they mean to others. When my marriage was new, my husband and I made a decision to move to New England. A job was set up with a great trucking company, and my family would be close to help me when our child made his entrance into the world. Unexpectedly, the job took a bit longer to come through. My husband had to accept a job that took him away from home from early morning until well after ten o'clock on most nights. It was a struggle, especially with the bills still getting tighter, but neither of us complained.

One night I came across an old recipe book I'd

borrowed from my grandmother. I opened to a page with a potato soup recipe. My husband loved potato soup, and I saw an opportunity to do something special for him. I danced around the kitchen gathering the ingredients for this small labor of love, taking care so it would be perfect.

I saw the headlights of our beat-up car as he pulled into the driveway, and quickly I set his bowl of soup with a stack of saltines on the side. I watched him come up the stairs obviously exhausted, but a big smile appeared on his face when he saw the soup. His eyes twinkled as he looked at me (I thought it was a little much for soup), and he saw my confusion. He softly stated, "Jamie, I don't know why you do this. I don't get to take you out or go to your appointments. I'm so tired most of the time; I know we aren't getting any time together, but still you stay up and wait for me with a smile and a fresh, hot dinner. Why?"

"Because I love you."

He seemed surprised by my simple answer, and I was surprised by his sentiment. It never occurred to me a small act of love and appreciation could create such an emotion, but it is God who inspires me to love. Who could expect less from God?

*Lord, as Samuel said, "Speak, for your servant is listening" (1 Samuel 3:10 NIV), I ask that You continue to lead me in ways to demonstrate Your love by looking after the needs of others.*

## Potato S

Cookware needed: large 2-qua.

Ingredients:
1 1/2 cups water
3 cups diced potatoes
1/2 cup diced celery
1/2 cup diced onion
2 chicken bullion cubes
1/2 teaspoon salt
2 cups milk
1 cup sour cream
Chopped chives
2 tablespoons flour

Directions: Combine water, potatoes, celery, onion, bullion, and salt. Cook until potatoes are tender. Cool for 20 minutes. Add 1 cup of milk. Heat. Mix sour cream, chives, remaining milk, and flour. Add mixture to the pot slowly; heat and serve. Optional: Add pieces of ham and sprinkle with grated cheese. Serves 4.

Cooking Tip: When making potato soup, allow potatoes and water to cool before adding milk.

**Jamie Meredith** is from New England and lives with her husband and three children in Kansas. She is currently working on her first fiction novel.

# Louisa's Feast

**by Armené Humber**

*"I am the bread of life. He who comes to me
will never go hungry, and he who believes in
me will never be thirsty."*
JOHN 6:35 NIV

E eeeet!" Cousin Louisa insisted, smiling and nodding as she deftly made room on my plate for one more dolma. Before I could protest, she topped off my glass with homemade apricot juice. "Drink—it!" she urged.

It wasn't as though I might starve. In fact, as I stared at my plate, I wondered how I could possibly ingest what lay before me—mushroom, potato, and beet salads, roasted potatoes, meatballs, fried cauliflower, okra- and zucchini-stuffed grape leaf dolmas, a stack of lavosh flatbread, two desserts, and fresh fruit!

"I—make—it—for—you," she beamed in her best broken English. Her radiant expression announced that she hadn't simply cooked this lavish

Armenian feast, she had *loved* it into existence.

What enormous work it must have been to prepare without the appliances I considered basic. Her efforts showed in her weary arthritic limp and on her hands, stained red from the pomegranate seeds she had scooped for garnish. And at what cost had she gathered this food! Since the end of Soviet rule in Armenia, this branch of my family had suffered enormous financial hardship. I couldn't imagine the sacrifice this meal represented.

Yet love gushed freely over the table, crowded with assorted cousins, aunts, uncles, grandparents, parents, and children, each out-shouting the other in an effort to be heard. Laughter and chatter gridlocked hopelessly over our heads as glasses clinked in joyous celebration of family reunited.

I had replayed this scene countless times since returning home in an effort to preserve it forever. Even on this Sunday in church, as the music played softly, I closed my eyes, aching to touch that warmth and abundance once more. But the miles between California and Armenia had dimmed its reality.

Then, from the front of the church, I heard familiar words. "Take. . . Eat. . . Drink." Here it was, an invitation to the table of ultimate sacrifice and unsurpassed love! A superabundant feast God had *loved* into reality—for *me*. He was offering, in this Eucharistic meal, all the warmth and love I had tasted at Louisa's table, and more—so much more.

All I had to do was eat.

*Oh, Lord, our precious Bread of Heaven, what*
*sacrifice You have made of Your own flesh and*
*blood so that we might have abundant life!*
*Help us never to take for granted the privilege*
*of gathering at Your table of Communion. And*
*keep us faithful 'til we all meet together at the*
*wedding feast of the Lamb.*

## Tahnabour
### (Armenian Yogurt Soup)

Tahnabour is a simple, but delicious, traditional soup served in most regions of Armenia. It is said to aid digestion and is often fed to those with a troubled stomach.

Cookware needed: 2-quart stovetop pan

Ingredients:
1 cup #3 bulgur (skinless whole)
4 cups water
1 teaspoon salt
16 ounces frozen chopped spinach
     (or 2 pounds fresh spinach, finely chopped)*
48 ounces plain nonfat yogurt
     (one 32-ounce container plus one-half of another)

*Prepare spinach: If frozen, remove from package, chop even finer, and squeeze out water. If fresh, place spinach in pot with 2 tablespoons olive oil, and let simmer until spinach wilts.

Directions: Add water to bulgur and simmer on medium heat until soft. Allow a little water to remain, or add more water to make a thinner consistency. Add salt. Add prepared spinach to bulgur mixture. Slowly add yogurt and mix constantly over low heat until bulgur mixture is slightly thickened. Let simmer, or turn off and reheat when serving. Serves 4 to 6.

Topping: (Optional, but adds exquisite flavor and aroma)
1 large onion cut in long, thin slices
3–4 tablespoons olive oil
2 tablespoons finely chopped dry mint

Brown onion in hot olive oil on medium-high heat until dark brown. Add chopped dry mint to onions; set aside. Garnish top of soup with onion mixture.

Cooking Tip: A coffee grinder can be used to chop the dry mint leaves.

**Armené Humber** is a freelance writer and storyteller whose passion is to capture the stories of God's work in today's world. As a career counselor, she assists homeless and low-income clients recognize their potential and become productive in today's difficult workplace. Armené lives in California and is working toward a master's degree in Christian leadership at Fuller Theological Seminary.

# Splits or Grits?

**by Fran Caffey Sandin**

*"Do not despise this small beginning, for the eyes of the Lord rejoice to see the work begin."*
ZECHARIAH 4:10 TLB

One fall day my Swedish hubby from Chicago grinned and said, "I'd like some split pea soup with ham, just like Mama used to make."

Having grown up in rural east Texas, I'd never even heard of it, so in my best Southern drawl I suggested, "Honey, how about some black-eyed peas instead?"

"Black-eyed peas?" Jim asked with a quizzical expression. "Isn't that cow feed?"

I bristled defensively, placed my hands on my hips, and firmly announced, "Well, not where I'm from!"

"I'm really hungry for some split pea soup!" Jim insisted.

As a new bride, eager to please, I finally said, "Then I'll just buy some and learn how to make it."

So I courageously added "split peas" to my shopping list.

I had three cooking pans—small, medium, and large. I started with the smallest one, but after adding water and cooking awhile, the thick soup almost overflowed. So I took out the next size up, added more water, but when I raised the lid, the peas had doubled! That was it! I poured everything in the Dutch oven, added more water, but when those peas stopped expanding, the soup resembled a marshy swamp with a matching aroma. So I added a few ham chunks and prayed.

That evening I eagerly watched Jim's facial expression, but after his first bite, I knew it wasn't Mama's. Still, he was kind enough to fake his approval to the bottom of the bowl. With our financial code of "use it up, wear it out, make it do, or do without," we ate split pea soup until we were sick of it.

I could have refused to try and cook the soup. He could have refused to eat it! But in my small way to please him and his small way to encourage me, we took another step in building our relationship. "Do not despise the day of small things." We are celebrating our fortieth wedding anniversary soon, and, looking back, our relationship could easily have "split" over a cup of soup.

*Dear Father, help us to realize that our*
*relationships are built little by little by the*
*choices we make. Help us to sacrificially love*

*and serve one another, ev*
*feel like it. Let us remember*
*the seemingly insignificant*
*ultimately impact us the*

## Navy Bean Soup
(A winter soup we both enjo)

Cookware needed: large stovetop kettle or Dutch oven

Ingredients:
2 cups dry navy beans
2 quarts water
1 1/2-pound ham bone
1 large onion, chopped
3 carrots, diced
3 ribs celery, leaves and all
1/4 cup bell pepper, chopped
1 can stewed tomatoes
2 cloves, whole
1 medium jalapeno pepper, finely chopped
Salt and pepper, to taste
Add extra chunks of ham, as desired

Directions: Wash beans, add water, cover, and soak overnight. Pour off water, rinse beans, and add 2 quarts fresh water. Cook on low heat with ham bone and onion until beans are tender. (I've never timed the steps because I like the flavors to "season" for several hours.) Add other ingredients and simmer until

...k occasionally, could take at least another ...Up to 3 jalapenos can be added if you like the ...xtra spicy flavor. This is a great recipe to use after the holiday ham is finished. Single bowl portions can be frozen for use later on. The aroma of this hearty soup is great! We like it with fresh-baked, hot corn bread and a salad. Serves: 8 to 10.

Cooking Tip: Soak dry beans or peas overnight in water. Then pour through a strainer to remove the water. Rinse beans or peas with fresh water (this decreases undesirable effects in the digestive system) and add the designated amount of water for cooking.

---

**Fran Caffey Sandin** is a grandmother, registered nurse, church organist, author, and speaker living in Greenville, Texas. Her books include *See You Later, Jeffrey* (Tyndale House) and *Touching the Clouds: Encouraging Stories to Make Your Faith Soar* (NavPress).

# Relaxing Respite

**by Deborah Wells**

*A generous man will prosper;*
*he who refreshes others will himself be refreshed.*
PROVERBS 11:25 NIV

My husband and I had just begun new-member classes at our church when they asked for volunteers to open their homes and host get-acquainted pot-luck dinners for class members to meet the pastoral staff. We both eagerly raised our hands along with two other couples.

During the following week, a major upheaval occurred in our church, causing a beloved pastoral member to resign. It was painful, and the burden on the remaining staff was overwhelming.

The first potluck went on as scheduled, but it was a quiet evening, not much laughter, as we were all still getting over the shock of what had transpired. The dinner was at the home of a couple about our age. I could see that great time and effort had gone into its decor as there were lovely dried floral sprays above the doorways; the furniture and picture placements and special heirloom pieces were magnificent. Afterward I commented to my husband that I couldn't believe we raised our hands to volunteer. Although our home was a nice and fairly new one, it certainly wasn't a decorator's show house. I fretted over all that needed to be done to bring our humble abode "up to par."

While preparing an appetizer the day before it was our turn to be hosts, the Lord gently showed me that in my worry, I had allowed the enemy to rob me of all joy in serving Him. My lack of contentment with what God had entrusted me with had caused my motive and focus for entertaining to become misplaced.

I prayed that the Lord would forgive me and help me to see things through His eyes. My goal became making my home an inviting and relaxing respite for those who were to come the next evening.

The house was cleaned, candles glowed, and soft Christian music played as our fellowship began. Upon his arrival, our associate pastor walked into our family room. From his mouth to my ears I heard him say, "Ahh, this is so inviting," as he stretched out his arms and relaxed.

*Father, I thank You for the joy and privilege*
*of serving You. Please help me to be content*
*with where You have placed me so that I*

*don't miss opportunities to bring glory*
*and honor to Your holy, precious name.*

## Smoked Salmon Spread

Ingredients:
1 (8-ounce) package cream cheese, softened
3 tablespoons sliced green onions (using some of
the green part)
1 (7-ounce—approximate size) can of sockeye
Salmon
3 drops liquid smoke
1/2 cup chopped fresh parsley

Directions: Soften cream cheese and combine with the green onions and salmon. Add liquid smoke and combine well. Chill for at least 8 hours or overnight for best flavor. Once firmer, this may be shaped into a ball and rolled in parsley for garnish. Sometimes I serve it in a dish with less parsley sprinkled on top for garnish. Serve with crackers.

Cooking Tip: Before adding the salmon to the cream cheese, break it up with your fingers and remove any of the small pieces of cartilage.

**Deborah Wells** is married and the mother of two teenagers. She is an avid cook who enjoys reading and writing. She resides in Greer, South Carolina.

# Some Left Over

### by Cathee A. Poulsen

*"Now then, what do you have on hand? Give me five
loaves of bread, or whatever you can find."*
1 SAMUEL 21:3 NIV

*W*hat can I fix for supper? It was Wednesday
night, and I stood at the refrigerator, willing inspiration to overtake me. I had popped a nicely seasoned
chicken in the oven, but that would hardly feed my
large family. The phone jarred me out of my reverie.
It was my husband, Bob.

"Listen, honey. Bill and Alma just called. Their
car broke down on I-75. I'll pick them up and bring
them for dinner. We can eat while their car's being
repaired and catch up on news."

"Sure thing. That's fine," I managed as panic
rose. Tomorrow was grocery day and the pickings
were sparse. Somehow I knew God would stretch
the meal. I prayed for wisdom to use the supplies on

87

hand and set to work.

I found two halves of French bread in the back of the freezer—*ah, garlic bread*. Frozen strawberries and half a pound cake I'd brought home from the church supper surfaced for dessert. Instead of baking potatoes, I thinly sliced and layered them into a casserole with onion and cheddar cheese. Voilà—scalloped potatoes! There were lots of green beans left from Monday's dinner.

Everyone came in as I finished setting the table. My six-foot-seven teenage son arrived from basketball practice. "Hey, Mom, what's for dinner?" His eyes lit up as he looked at the golden baked chicken, scalloped potatoes, green beans, and garlic bread.

We took seats and bowed our heads as Bob thanked God for our meal. I silently breathed one more prayer that God would stretch that chicken.

The evening passed quickly with a delicious meal and conversation about old times with good friends. We laughed, ate, and sipped coffee with the pound cake and strawberries.

It wasn't until they left and I was clearing the table that I noticed a drumstick and thigh still on the platter. *Imagine that*. Not only had God answered my prayer, there was even some left over.

*Father, help me to trust You with all my*
*circumstances—not only the times of crisis but*

*also in the little frustrations and surprises of
life. You are my Provider in all things.*

### Scalloped Potatoes
Preheat oven: 350° F.
Cookware needed: large stovetop pot,
skillet, large casserole dish

Ingredients:
2 cups half-and-half or light cream
1 clove garlic, thinly sliced
2 tablespoons Dijon mustard
3 cups potatoes, peeled and thinly sliced
2 tablespoons unsalted butter
1 cup onions, thinly sliced
Salt, to taste
1/2 teaspoon freshly ground black pepper
Fresh parsley, chopped

Directions: Bring the cream and the garlic to a
boil in a large saucepan. Reduce the heat and simmer
until reduced by a third, 5 to 8 minutes. Add mustard
and mix well. Set aside.

Fill a large pot with water and bring to a boil.
Drop in the peeled, sliced potatoes and blanch for
30 seconds. Drain, rinse under cold water, and dry
on paper towels. Melt the butter in a skillet and cook
the onions on low heat until translucent. In a large
casserole dish, layer the potatoes and onions, sprinkling lightly with salt and pepper. Top with the cream

sauce and sprinkle with fresh parsley, if desired. (If it seems dry, add a little more cream.) Bake for 1 hour.

Place under the broiler a few minutes until the top is brown and bubbly. Serves 6.

Cooking Tip: When making soup, stew, or even scalloped potatoes, you can slice the potatoes and skip peeling them. The dish will be easier to prepare and more nutritious.

**Cathee Poulsen** is a speaker, leader, and freelance writer living in Naples, Florida. She is the mother of four and grandmother of seven, living the great adventure and telling her stories to bring encouragement and hope to others.

# His Love Is Enough

**by Lindsey Renfroe**

*I was young and now I am old,*
*yet I have never seen the righteous forsaken*
*or their children begging bread.*
PSALM 37:25 NIV

It's become a running joke in our house: "So, umm, what else are we having?"

This is the question my husband would ask upon looking at the dinner I had painstakingly prepared for him. The problem wasn't that we couldn't afford food, but being married only a short time, I needed to rewire my brain to determine the proper portion sizes that would feed two people. When I had cooked for my parents and sisters before I was married, I prepared enough to feed five or more people, so at the beginning of our marriage, we had so much left-over food, it would spoil before we could finish it.

When I tried making smaller portions, it was

never enough to satisfy us, and we would find ourselves making an extra ham sandwich when the original meal was consumed. The frustration grew as I
began experimenting with the menu. My husband
and I were rarely on the same page when it came to
tastes in food. When he wanted barbecue, I wanted
burritos.

I was a new wife and wanted more than anything to have a satisfied husband. The thought that
my husband was still hungry or would not enjoy what
I had prepared was devastating to me. Interestingly
enough, my husband will tell you that he has never
gone hungry or felt like he's missed a meal. And he
will probably tell you that he appreciates every meal
that has been cooked for him.

We can view God's provision in a very similar
way. Just as easily, *we* can miss the blessing of a carefully prepared meal because it doesn't look like it
could possibly be enough to satisfy our hunger. We
may also find ourselves saying: "So, umm, Lord, what
*else* can You do for me?"

Sometimes what we wish to happen is not what
God has prepared for us. But God promises that He
will provide for us and we will be satisfied. "Look
at the birds of the air, they neither toil nor reap, yet
the heavenly Father feeds them. Are we not of more
value then they?"

*Father, thank You for Your*
*Your wonderful deeds. You*
*and fill our hunger wit*

### Broccoli-Raisin

Ingredients:
2 stalks fresh broccoli
1 cup celery, chopped
1 cup raisins
1/2 cup walnuts
1/2 cup sunflower seeds (optional)

Dressing:
1 cup mayonnaise or Miracle Whip
1/4 cup vinegar
1/4 cup sugar

Directions: Cut flowerets from broccoli stalks and break into small pieces. Mix with chopped celery, raisins, walnuts, and sunflower seeds. Mix mayonnaise with vinegar and sugar; pour over broccoli mix and refrigerate 30 minutes before serving. Serves 4 to 6.

Cooking Tip: Keep an airtight salad spinner (such as the OXO SoftWorks) full of mixed lettuce greens in the refrigerator as a healthy side dish for any meal. Salad is also a great snack for between meals.

...nfroe is wife of Will, mother of handsome twin ...den and Maddux, and a beautiful daughter, Riley. ...n finishing her undergraduate degree, she plans to be-...ome a cosmetologist and eventually serve on the mission field.

# Beef, Chicken, Fish, and Elk!

# Tough or Tender

**by Dianne E. Butts**

*Today, if you hear his voice, do not harden your
hearts as you did at Meribah, as you did that
day at Massah in the desert.*
PSALM 95:7–8 NIV

When preparing meats for our dinner, we look
for tender cuts. But I've learned a good marinade
will tenderize even the toughest of meats before
cooking.

While we may admire the hard, muscular bodies of male and female athletes and celebrities, the
spiritual heart is one muscle that we don't want to be
tough in anyone. A hard spiritual heart can be deadly
because it resists both the affection of those near and
the tender calling of our loving Savior.

I once had a heart that was hard toward the Lord.
When I had questions about God and could find no
satisfactory answers, I decided there were none, and

my heart grew hard. When tragedy struck, I wondered why a caring God would let it happen, and my heart hardened more. When I expected people in my life to behave a certain way and they failed, I decided love was all just a sham. My heart grew harder still.

But I was not alone in the hard-heart department. Moses performed God's miracles, but even miracles did not soften Pharaoh's hard heart. The Israelites' hearts grew hard as they quarreled with Moses and grumbled against the Lord at Meribah. The apostle Paul's hard heart would not believe Jesus was the Christ until he met the resurrected Lord on the road to Damascus.

Today, I'm surrounded by people whose hearts are hard toward others and the Lord. Sometimes it seems their hearts are so hard that nothing could penetrate them—but then I remember when my own heart was just as hard.

A friend once told me every meat marinade has some kind of acid in it. As the muscle soaks in the marinade, the acid breaks down the fibers in tough cuts of meat, causing them to become tender. Jesus is like a sweet marinade for our hearts, patiently basting us in His mercy and His grace. He doesn't give up. He pursues us, hoping we will soak in His love. If we do, our hearts become tender toward Him.

And when I spend enough time marinating in the love of Jesus, my life becomes a sweet marinade of love to others.

*Lord, wherever I encounter hearts that are hard toward You, help me to be a tenderizing marinade, surrounding them with Your sweet love and grace and mercy, gently helping them soften their hearts so they may accept You.*

## Flank Steak Marinated in Teriyaki Sauce
Cookware needed: oven broiler or outdoor grill

Ingredients:
1/3 cup olive oil
1/3 cup vegetable oil
1/3 cup soy sauce
Juice of one lemon (this is the acid)
 (Juice concentrate from a bottle works fine.)
1/2 onion, chopped
1 garlic clove, crushed
1 flank steak

Directions: Mix all ingredients in a flat glass dish. Add flank steak, cover with plastic wrap, and refrigerate at least 4 hours (overnight is better). Turn steak regularly so both sides are marinated. Broil steak to desired doneness (approximately 8 to 10 minutes per side).

Cooking Tip: Cut meat across the grain in thin strips, holding the knife at an angle, for an attractive way to serve.

**Dianne E. Butts'** heart became tender toward the Lord in her midtwenties. A writer since 1989, she desires to share why believing in Jesus Christ is logical and reasonable. When she's not writing or cooking for her husband, Hal, she spends time in her flower garden with her cat, P.C., or riding her motorcycle.

# Help, Lord, I Married a Hunter!

**by Becky Weber**

*"He who finds his life will lose it,
and he who loses his life for My sake will find it."*
MATTHEW 10:39 NKJV

When Scott and I were first married, I didn't understand the passion he had for hunting, but I soon discovered that I lived with an avid hunter. Every fall, my wonderful husband transformed into a passionate huntsman in eager pursuit of his kill and blessed his family with an abundance of meat.

At first, the taste of the meat didn't appeal to me, and I had no idea how to cook it. I felt trapped and even resentful at Scott's expectation that I should enjoy this wild game he proudly provided for his family. I desperately needed an attitude change, so I asked God to help me. Then I realized that I simply needed to disguise the wild-game taste. This was a challenge, but one I have successfully accomplished by adding sauces and seasonings to the meat.

Now every year when Scott's hunt is complete, I prepare a feast of deer or elk meat as a celebration dinner in honor of his success! One year, I decided to humorously display my hunter's conquest by placing his deer antlers as a centerpiece on our dinner table. Elaborate candles on both sides displayed his prize antlers in all their glory.

When Scott came home, he saw the atmosphere as romantically charged for his arrival. I meant the centerpiece as a joke, but my husband was delighted! Rushing upstairs, he grabbed the camera to take a picture of this hunter's dream table.

Watching Scott's response, I realized how what I intended to be a joke had turned out to be a creative expression of love. This gesture of celebration deeply touched Scott's heart and inspired a cherished memory between us. Now, after thirty-six years of marriage, I'm still learning unique ways to reach my husband's heart and celebrate the gift he is to me. Through a few candles and a sense of humor, God showed me that sometimes loving another person requires sacrificing my own tastes—but the benefits keep me in abundant supply.

*Father, teach me more creative ways*
*to celebrate the ones I love and*
*demonstrate Your love for them.*

## Venison (or Elk) Swiss Steak
Cookware needed: Crock-Pot or slow cooker

Ingredients:
1 teaspoon Worcestershire sauce
Dash pepper
1 cup onions and mushrooms, sliced
1/2 cup green peppers, chopped
1 pound elk or venison meat, cut into pieces
1 cup water
2 teaspoons Wyler's Beef Granules
1 large can crushed tomatoes
1/2 cup sour cream

Directions: Place all ingredients, except sour cream, inside Crock-Pot greased with nonstick cooking spray. Cook on high for 1 hour. Cook on low approximately 6 hours, until meat is tender. Add sour cream and serve over noodles or mashed potatoes.

Cooking Tip: A Crock-Pot is the best way to cook venison or elk meat. Slow-cooking preserves the juices, and the meat remains tender and moist.

**Becky Weber** is a freelance Christian writer and founder of Fragrance Ministries. She speaks and writes booklets addressing issues of the heart to bring restoration and healing through the blood of Christ. Becky and her husband, Scott, reside in Coeur d'Alene, Idaho, and have three grown children and six grandchildren.

# Precious Recipes

**by Marilyn Black**

*You have made known to me the path of life;*
*you will fill me with joy in your presence,*
*with eternal pleasures at your right hand.*
PSALM 16:11 NIV

One year we were given a Bible that was 120 years old. The pages were crisp and the binding flawless, but rarely used except for a page recording the births, deaths, and marriages. This living Word, kept precious under beautiful gold and leather binding, is a valuable antique now. My Bible will never be a valuable antique. Its pages are limp and words underlined, its black leather cover is worn to a dull gray. In contrast, it is not an expensive ornament used only for special occasions; it is opened frequently to reveal the Word by which I live.

Like my old Bibles, some of my recipe books have glossy covers and remain unused, but my battered

*Hostess Recipe Book* is as precious to me as the family photo albums. For over thirty years, the recipes of friends and family members have been entered onto its pages, making it both an autograph album and travelogue of places I have visited throughout the world. Names and dates headline each recipe, and some are written in the giver's hand.

Through its pages, I can see the journey that my life has taken, starting with Bev's casserole given to me as a nervous young bride. She was an older Christian woman who was both mentor and friend to me, giving me recipes that I cautiously tested on my new husband. I would often cook the same recipe until I had the confidence to entertain family members and friends with it. Slowly the heart-thumping fear of failure quieted to a steady, natural rhythm as I learned that the recipe would not fail.

My cookbook journey has become more elaborate through the years. I can see the dinner parties, birthdays, and anniversary recipes as my family has grown, and with it my confidence to undertake large catering assignments. My spiritual growth with the Lord has taken the same path as my favorite recipe book. When I turn to a page in my tattered Bible, I can see an underlined scripture that inspires my Christian walk, and knowing it will not fail me because I have tested it many times, I have confidence to step out and use it again.

*Lord, let the days of my life be filled with
the wisdom of time-tested recipes and Your
unfailing truth, so that the rhythm of my
heart remains steady and sure.*

### Bev's Sweet and Sour Steak
(I name each recipe after the person who gave it to me.)

Cookware needed: large sauté pan.

Ingredients:
1 teaspoon butter or oil
1 pound (500 g) blade steak, cut into cubes
1 medium onion, sliced
1 tablespoon soy sauce
1 tablespoon fruit chutney
1 medium can sliced pineapple*
1 tablespoon corn flour (cornstarch)
3 tablespoons water

*Optional: Peaches can be used instead of pineapple.

Directions: Place oil or butter in pan and brown the meat. Add sliced onion and brown. Add soy sauce, chutney, and the juice from the pineapple. Cook about 1 hour on a low heat until meat is tender. Thicken with corn flour mixed with water and add pineapple pieces to just heat through. Serves 4.

Cooking Tip: Use the wrappers from sticks of butter to grease cookie sheets and baking pans.

**Marilyn Black** is married to David, and they have three adult children and seven grandchildren. They live in an old farmhouse in the country with six acres of New Zealand land where they raise a few cows. Marilyn has a women's wear shop in a nearby town.

# Comfort Foods

### by Joan E. B. Coombs

*Moses said. . .It is the bread (comfort food)*
*that the LORD has given you to eat.*
EXODUS 16:15, AUTHOR'S PARAPHRASE

The best definition for "comfort food" isn't found on the pages of *Webster's Unabridged Dictionary*. It's found on tables or kitchen counters, in oven-to-table plates, travel dishes, and Crock-Pots. It is meals and desserts attractively arrayed on buffet tables in a fellowship or dining hall.

I've learned from God that there is ministry in baking, cooking, and providing comfort foods. When words escape us, our kitchen creations say, "I love you and care about your needs."

As a young mother of two young children, I was hospitalized, had surgery twice within three months, and then faced restrictions in recovery. In short order, I received comfort food's ministry. Meals, salads, and desserts from neighbors and church friends became my family's mainstay. These servant-saints showed love in action.

Later, amid the joys of raising "tween-agers," the ensuing years also brought the sad, earthly loss of a special family member. One chilly February afternoon, Grandad Coombs wept through his phone call: "Mom had an aneurysm at work." Within minutes our family of four packed suitcases, and within hours flew from snow-crusted New England to Pittsburgh, Pennsylvania.

The hospital ICU team offered no hope. Our daily around-the-clock watch changed to making funeral plans and ended helping a widower walk through sudden shock, loss, and incredible grief.

During our desolate times, heaven-sent comfort food arrived from neighbors, church friends, and parcel post! That "minidesert, nomadic experience" somewhat paralleled the Old Testament story of when God sent sweet-tasting manna to His displaced people.

Years later, I'm still learning that kitchen cooks have a unique "Manna Ministry." Comfort food (whether cooked, baked, or hand-tossed with love) brings honey to the hurting. And, as this bread of heaven reaches deeply into their souls, it shows the wounded that they are loved.

*God, our Father, thank You*
*daily bread. We praise You*
*resources to serve others for t*
*glory. Help us to minister w*
*bring comfort into the l*

# New England-Style Cranb——— ———————

(Have portable bakeware, will travel!)

Cookware needed: Crock-Pot

Ingredients:
1 large bag frozen precooked meatballs
(96 mini-sized)
2 cans whole berry cranberry sauce
1 can cranberry sauce (1 more if you prefer
more sauce)
1 to 2 12-ounce bottles Heinz (or store brand)
chili sauce
Mix cranberries and sauce ingredients. Put in
Crock-Pot to simmer.

Directions: Defrost meatballs in the microwave. Drain fat. Mix meatballs in stirred, simmering cranberry-chili sauce mixture. Simmer 3 to 4 hours (or more) for best marinated taste. Servings: approximately 30. Optional: Serve with party toothpicks.

Tip: If you have an urgent ministry comfort food, this same recipe can be by simmering the sauce mixture atop the stove, thawing the meatballs, and then letting them simmer in the cranberry-chili sauce mixture until you have to dash out the door!

**Joan E. B. Coombs** is a happily married wife, mother, and grandmother. She enjoys the ministries of writing and serving her Lord, her family, her local church, and her friends with gladness. She cofounded "Scribes 'n' Scribblers," a Western Massachusetts Christian Writers' Fellowship.

# Chili—In the Pocket?

### by Linda J. Gilden

*No one has ever seen God; but if we love one another,*
*God lives in us and his love is made complete in us.*
1 JOHN 4:12 NIV

Mom, what's that smell?" asked Lalsiamkimi, our exchange student from India. I was putting the finishing touches on supper as she came into the house from school. Obviously, the smell from the kitchen had greeted her at the door.

"Chili," I replied, my face beaming at this culinary labor of love. I had never made chili before and studied several cookbooks before deciding on a recipe for my daughter. "You said the other day you loved to eat chili in your country. Doesn't chili smell like this in India?"

"Chili doesn't smell at all until you get your nose very close to it. Chilies are green and very hot. I like to carry one in my pocket and eat it! You just bite off a little at a time."

"Carry it in your. . ? Uh-oh, I guess I goofed, didn't I?" I chuckled at my blunder.

"Goofed?" Kim (our shortened version of Lalsiamkimi) said with a puzzled expression. She was so cute when she wrinkled up her nose.

"I made a mistake. I goofed!"

There were many phrases and words that we used every day that were new to Kim. And many of the customs in our country were different, too. During the year Kim lived with us, we learned many new things about India and those who lived there. They ate different foods, they worshiped differently, and they dressed in different clothing.

But we also learned we had things in common. Though we came from countries that were a world apart, we loved the same God. And His love is far greater than any cultural or culinary differences we may encounter. When our family sings "Jesus loves the little children, all the children of the world," we know it is true.

Even though Kim has gone back to India, we talk about her often. And we will never forget those beautiful brown eyes and sweet smile or the "proper" way (in India, of course!) to eat a chili.

*Lord, thank You that Your love transcends culture, culinary, and every other type of difference we find between ourselves and*

*others. Help us to cling to the common bond of
Your love as we try to understand our friends
who may be different from us. Your love is
really the only thing we need. Amen.*

## Chili for a Crowd
(from the kitchen of Kristi Gilden Bowen)

Kristi is my oldest daughter who spent many happy
times with Lalsiamkimi. Now that she is married and
loves to cook, her chili is "famous" in our family,
especially with her younger brother and his friends.
Often they will ask her, "Hey, Kristi, when are we
coming to your house for chili again?"

Cookware needed: Crock-Pot or slow cooker

Ingredients:
2 pounds ground beef
1 medium onion, chopped
1 bell pepper, chopped
1/2 pound kidney beans, not drained
2 tablespoons chili powder
1 teaspoon cumin
2 (1-pound) cans tomatoes
1/4 teaspoon minced garlic
Salt, to taste

Directions: Brown meat. When it starts browning, add onions. Toward the end of browning, add

peppers. Put in slow cooker. Add remaining ingredients. Let simmer overnight. Serves 10 to 12.

Cooking Tip: Chili is best when served with lots of grated cheese and sour cream. Or, if you prefer, provide salad greens and corn chips to create a taco salad.

**Linda Gilden** is a full-time freelance writer. Her newest book is *Love Notes in Lunchboxes* (New Hope Publishers). Teaching at national writers' conferences, Linda likes helping people discover and develop their writing talent. She enjoys family time where she finds lots of inspiration for her writing.

# Never-Ending Family Feast

**by Cynthia Agricola Hinkle**

*"I have come that they may have life,
and have it to the full."*
JOHN 10:10 NIV

I grew up in an extended Filipino family near San Francisco. We gathered for dinner every birthday and holiday. Filipino dinner parties were never bound to a clock, so my relatives showed up hours late—then stayed hours later.

Each family brought gifts and food. The dinner table groaned from platters of ham, roast pork, chicken, beef, and fish with glazed eyes. Garnishing the meats were fruits, potatoes, green salads, egg rolls, and *pancit*, a Filipino noodle dish. Noodles represented a wish for long life for the birthday honoree.

During the feasting, the uncles joked, while aunties and cousins sang at the piano or into a karaoke mike. Chatter was animated—a spicy mix of English,

Spanish, and Tagalog phrases. Our hearts warmed as tummies filled.

Years later my heart ached under an icy gray Pennsylvania sky. It was a week before Christmas and not one relative could visit us, even though December twenty-fifth was my husband's birth date. I was so depressed, I hadn't even planned Christmas dinner for our three children or a birthday cake for my husband, Andy.

Then my church friend Laura called, telling me that she and her husband Paul had to cancel plans to visit their grandkids. They would probably eat Christmas dinner at a restaurant. As I put the phone down, the Lord gently whispered, "Family's here." After I talked with my husband, I called Laura back.

I still hadn't cooked the noodles when our friends arrived Christmas night, thirty minutes early. They came bearing gifts and a homemade cherry chocolate cake for Andy. While I served spaghetti and Italian Roast Beef, everyone chatted, laughed, then sang a noisy "Happy Birthday."

Heart and tummy filled, I got a glimpse of heaven's banquet where believing friends and family chat, giggle, and sing in a thousand languages. Maybe heaven's Host will serve platters of noodles stretching to eternity. For one Christmas birthday long ago, Jesus came to live, die, and rise up so we would have more than a wish for long life—He gave us life, forever loved, forever full.

*Dear God, sometimes we forget Your love is forever near us. Your Word says in Psalm 68:6 that You set "the lonely in families, [and lead] forth the prisoners with singing"(NIV). Cause Your love to pour through us and help us to invite others to Your eternal love feast.*

## Italian Roast Beef and Spaghetti

Provide a shaker of Parmesan cheese,
a leafy salad, and enjoy with company.

Cookware needed: Crock-Pot or slow cooker

Ingredients:
3 to 4 pounds beef rump roast, fat trimmed
1 medium onion, diced
1 (4-ounce) can mushrooms stems and
    pieces, drained
1 envelope Italian spaghetti sauce mix
1 to 2 (8-ounce) cans tomato sauce
1 large green pepper, diced, set aside
Thin spaghetti noodles

Directions: Grease a large Crock-Pot with olive oil. Set trimmed meat into pot. In a medium bowl, mix the chopped onion, drained mushrooms, spaghetti sauce dry mix, and tomato sauce. Pour over meat. Cover and cook on low for 8 to 9 hours. In the last hour of cooking, add the diced pepper and boil water for the noodles. Carve the meat into thin slices for a platter. Pour the chunky sauce into a bowl. In a separate warmed serving bowl, place the cooked noodles and toss with a dash of olive oil. Serves 8.

Cooking Tip: After removing the cooked meat from the pot, the sauce may be thickened by adding a little cornstarch dissolved in 1/4 cup cold water.

Mom to Michael, Jessica, and Peter, **Cynthia Agricola Hinkle** is a freelance writer and author who loves hosting noisy parties after the preparation is over. She has authored *Star of Wonder*, a children's Christmas book, available in 2005.

# More Than a Bucket of Chicken

**by Cheri Lynn Cowell**

*We proclaim to you what we have seen and heard, so
that you also may have fellowship with us. And our
fellowship is with the Father and with his Son,
Jesus Christ. We write this to make our joy complete.*

1 JOHN 1:3–4 NIV

I remember when covered-dish dinners were more
than a bucket of fried chicken or deli salad. They
were where you could get the best home cookin'
from some of the best cooks around. Everyone
would bring their signature dishes, the ones for
which the recipes were always requested. My father
loved covered-dish dinners so much that he volun-
teered to help in the kitchen just so he could get a
good look at everything.

One of my favorite dishes at those dinners was
Granny Nell's Spaghetti Pie. Now she wasn't my real
grandma, but she treated me as if I were her own. If

for some reason I wasn't at the covered-dish dinner, she would save a large piece of her "pie" just for me. When as an adult I began to make this dish, it never seemed to taste the same. Eventually, I understood it wasn't the recipes that made those covered dishes so great—it was the sense of belonging that made everything taste so good.

As I compared the fellowship dinners of my childhood with those of today, I realized that true fellowship happens when there is more than just being together. It is more than just having something in common, or even enjoying each other's company. True fellowship is when there is a spiritual and social connection. Fellowship is interacting, even noticing when someone isn't present, as Grandma Nell noticed when I wasn't there to receive my favorite serving of her love.

Said another way, true fellowship happens when we are intentional about loving, as Christ loves, those with whom we are sharing a meal. This sometimes means putting our needs aside and listening to someone else, and other times it means serving and looking after others—just because.

Now, every time I make spaghetti pie, I am reminded to focus on the people in my life. I take special care to reach deeper than just social conversation. I strive to connect on a spiritual level to those whom I am serving, and as I do, I know Granny Nell is smiling from that big kitchen in the sky.

*Dear heavenly Father, thank You for
the opportunity to serve those I love. Help
me to be more focused on people than
preparations as we share time of fellowship.*

## Spaghetti Pie

Preheat oven to 300° F.
Cookware needed: greased 9-inch pie plate

Ingredients:
8 ounces thin spaghetti, cooked and drained
6 ounces ground mild Italian sausage, browned
    and drained
3 ounces Parmesan cheese
15 ounces ricotta cheese
2 eggs, beaten
1/2 teaspoon Italian seasoning
2 cups garden-style spaghetti sauce
1 cup mozzarella cheese

Directions: Mix together the cooked spaghetti, sausage, Parmesan and ricotta cheeses, eggs, and Italian seasoning. Press the spaghetti mixture into a greased pie plate to form a crust. Pour the spaghetti sauce over the crust. Top with mozzarella cheese. Bake uncovered for 45 minutes; slightly cool and slice into wedges before serving. Serves 6.

Cooking Tip: To help you focus more on people than preparations at dinnertime, divide preparation roles amongst family members by writing assignments on cards or on a wipe-off board posted in the kitchen. Then as everyone is doing their assigned tasks, you can guide the conversation by focusing on the things in their lives that matter most.

In her popular "Recipes for Life" presentations, **Cheri Lynn Cowell** shares recipes for body and soul, a recurring theme in her writing and speaking ministry. "I love to share my favorite recipes with my audience while helping them to discover the recipe God gave for a life of peace, joy, and contentment."

# Don't Change the Recipe

**by Karen Hardin**

*The ordinances of the L*ORD *are sure and altogether righteous. They are more precious than gold, than much pure gold; they are sweeter than honey, than honey from the comb.*
PSALM 19:9–10 NIV

W hat do you think?" Regina asked as I began to chew the small white cookie. She leaned closer as I caught sight of her son, Patrick, shaking his head. My taste buds registered their complaint at the same time that my mind registered Patrick's reaction. This wasn't going to be good.

Regina was an amazing cook. We had become friends when my husband and I moved to China to teach English and share the gospel. In spite of our cultural differences, we became close friends. As time allowed she taught me the art of Chinese cooking, and I taught her how to bake in the small countertop ovens that had recently become available in their state-run stores.

Still waiting for my response, I noticed belatedly that neither Regina's husband nor her son were eating her "cookies." The hard concoction stuck in my throat as my mind raced for something kind to say.

"What did you put in them?" I asked, stalling.

"Well, I followed the recipe," she began, "except I cut out two-thirds of the sugar, one of the eggs, and substituted pig lard for butter."

*No wonder,* I thought as I washed the offensive bite down with a large gulp of hot tea. Afterward I thought about Regina's cookies. *"I followed the recipe. . . ,"* she had stated, but in reality she hadn't. Her changes had seemed logical at the time, but the end product was far from the desired result. It was then that I sensed God speaking to my heart.

"Isn't that what you do?"

*No way,* I thought. I had been cooking since I was very young. I would never have made those same changes.

And then I realized we weren't talking about cookies.

"I offer you instructions for your life from My Word, but as you make changes here and substitutions there, the final product will never be the sweet result that I planned."

Over the months, Regina's cookies improved as she learned where to tweak a recipe and where to follow it completely. And we both learned the importance of following God's Word, the recipe for our lives, exactly as He wrote it.

> *Dear God, help me to always follow*
> *Your "recipe" for my life rather than my own*
> *plan. Help me to learn to trust You that the*
> *end result will be a sweet savor in Your*
> *presence that brings You glory.*

## Tang Cu Li Ji
(Sweet and Sour Pork)

Cookware needed: large skillet or deep fryer

Ingredients:
1 pound pork (chicken also works well)
1 egg
4 tablespoons cornstarch
2 green onions
5 to 6 cloves garlic
2 teaspoons grated ginger
1/2 cup water
1 tablespoon white vinegar
1/2 cup sugar
2 to 3 carrots
Salt and pepper, to taste

Directions: Cut pork into strips, approximately 1 x 3 inches and very thin. Make a batter by mixing the egg with cornstarch. Add just enough water to stir easily. Add strips of meat to the batter and stir until well coated. Fry in very hot oil until lightly browned. Remove from heat and let drain on a paper towel. Remove excess oil.

Finely chop onions, garlic, and add ginger. Add to 3 tablespoons of hot oil and stir-fry lightly for approximately 1 minute. Add water, vinegar, and sugar. Bring to a boil. Add salt and pepper to taste. Add fried meat strips to the mixture along with sliced carrots, cut thinly on the diagonal. Cover and let simmer approximately 2 to 3 minutes. Finally add a little cornstarch and water mixture just to thicken the sauce. Once sauce has thickened, remove and serve with rice. Serves 4 to 6.

Cooking Tip: Chinese stir-fry often requires cutting meat into very thin strips. If the meat is cut too thick, it will not cook through in a quick stir-fry. For ease in preparation, freeze your meat in advance and then cut the meat into the thin strips while it is still partially frozen.

**Karen Hardin** is author of *Seasons of Life for Women*. In addition to writing, she is a seasoned missionary and busy mom. Her work has appeared in *USA Today*, *Charisma* magazine, and *Make Your Day Count for Teachers*. Her newest book is *Seasons of Love*, (Lakeland, FL: White Stone Books, 2005).

# Sunday Chicken

**by Ava Chambers**

*Do not be anxious about anything,*
*but in everything, by prayer and petition,*
*with thanksgiving, present your requests to God.*
PHILIPPIANS 4:6 NIV

Mama's words were always the same: "Hurry, honey! Change out of those church clothes so we can go to MeeMaw's for dinner." Every Sunday for most of my life we paraded home from church, changed into our play clothes, loaded into Daddy's truck, and headed to MeeMaw's house.

The main menu was always the same, too—chicken. Depending on the season, various fruits and vegetables graced the table. But there was always chicken. Fried, baked, stewed; there was always chicken. As I grew older, I got to where I didn't care for Sunday dinner much.

"Mama," I once grumbled, "why does MeeMaw

always have chicken?"

"It's her promise to God," Mama said.

Cocking my eyebrow, I sighed. Sensing a lecture was about to take place, I wished I hadn't asked Mama to explain.

"I was born in 1929," Mama said. "Those were hard times, and it seemed that more hard times were coming. My family struggled to eat. There was no hopping in the truck to get food from the store. We grew what we ate. And one week, what we grew was gone. Papa left to search for work, Mama was left with two little girls, no money, no phone, and no food."

"So, you're here. You obviously didn't starve to death," I said.

"No, MeeMaw fell to her knees on the kitchen floor. I remember standing behind her with my hands on her shoulders as she asked God to send food."

"And?"

"We looked out the window and a little hen walked through the yard. She found a bit of flour in the bin and made the finest chicken dinner we'd ever had."

Something inside my heart broke. I envisioned a little girl standing tall beside a mother who was at the end of her ability to care for her family. I felt ashamed of all the times I'd taken a meal for granted. I felt ashamed of a lot of things.

"MeeMaw vowed in that moment to honor God's bounty," Mama said. "That's why we always have chicken on Sunday."

All these years later, I stand in my kitchen listening to my children giggle and fuss as they change out of their church clothes.

"What's for dinner, Mama?" my son yells.

"Chicken," I answer.

*Dear Lord, please help me remember to be thankful for what I have and to know that You will lovingly provide for my needs when I ask.*

### Southern Fried Chicken
Cookware needed: cast-iron skillet

Ingredients:
4 cups oil
2 chicken breasts
Salt and pepper, to taste
1 to 1 1/2 cups flour

Directions: Heat oil in cast-iron skillet. Coat chicken in flour. Add salt and pepper. Put chicken in oil. (Oil should at least cover half of chicken piece.) Turn chicken over 3 or 4 times until evenly brown. A breast usually takes a minimum of 20 minutes to fry.

Cooking Tip: Drop a few pinches of flour in the heated oil to determine if the oil is hot enough to begin frying the meat. The flour should hop and dance, letting you know the oil is hot and the skillet is ready.

**Ava Chambers** is a mother of four who is living in Acworth, Georgia. She spends her time writing, working at church, and transporting children to various activities. Her first work of fiction, *Dundury: The Secret* is now available online and at fine bookstores.

# Tasty Dish Satisfies Ministry Wish

### by Mary E. McCloud

*I thank Christ Jesus our Lord, who has given me*
*strength, that he considered me faithful,*
*appointing me to his service.*
1 TIMOTHY 1:12 NIV

W hat's wrong?" my husband asked, seeing the serious look on my face.

"I keep thinking about today's sermon. It was about finding your ministry, and I don't know what our ministry is."

"We have a gumbo ministry," my other half replied. I smiled, realizing he was right.

Making a pot of chicken and sausage gumbo is a specialty at our house. After years of cooking and experimenting, we have perfected this Cajun cuisine. From stirring the roux to the last taste test, making this dish is both a science and an art.

Throughout the years, particularly after the first cold blast of autumn, we've prepared gumbo and invited folks into our home. Nothing can compare to sharing warm conversation and a bowl of homemade gumbo. Encouragement, discipleship, and fellowship blend so well with this tasty comfort food.

One time we were visiting friends in New Mexico, and we met their pastor, an older gentleman, and his wife. They told us how they had migrated from Texas to New Mexico, and that they were both raised in southeast Texas, near the Louisiana border.

"Do you like gumbo?" I asked. His smile and the gleam in his eye answered yes.

"Good. Why don't you join us tonight after church?"

Our friends telephoned some of their neighbors while my husband and I shopped, chopped, cooked, and stirred. After the midweek service, our friends' little house was full of people and a mouthwatering aroma. We served bowls of steaming gumbo amid the sounds of conversation and laughter.

Later, after the dishes were washed and put away and the last good-bye was said, the house was quiet once again. As we were reflecting on the enjoyable evening, our friends told us how they had made several unsuccessful attempts during the past year to get the neighborhood families together for a visit. They had almost given up, until they heard us offering to make a pot of gumbo for supper. This tasty dish paved the way for their neighbors to come over, relax, eat, and get better acquainted. It opened the door to their home, and hopefully, their hearts.

*Lord, thank You for giving us the insight to see cooking as a ministry, a labor that benefits others. Thank You for showing us that ministering to people isn't always found in a church program or journeying to a distant land, but it can be found here, in the comfort of our own homes.*

## Chicken and Sausage Gumbo
Cookware needed: large stovetop kettle

Ingredients:
1/2 cup peanut oil
1 cup all-purpose flour
1 cup onion, chopped
1 cup green onion, chopped
1/2 cup bell pepper, chopped
1/2 cup fresh parsley, chopped
1/4 cup celery, chopped
1 gallon chicken broth (reserved from
    boiling the chicken)
1 tablespoon garlic, chopped
1 can beef broth
1 small package frozen okra, thawed
1 whole chicken, boiled and deboned
1 pound smoked sausage, cut into 1/4-inch slices

1 tablespoon Worcestershire sauce
1 teaspoon Tony Chachere's Original Creole
    Mix Seasoning

Directions: Heat the oil in a large, heavy pot over medium heat, then add the flour. Cook on medium heat slowly as the roux changes from a cream color all the way to a dark chocolate color. Stir constantly to keep it from burning. This may take 30 to 45 minutes. To the roux, add the onion, green onion, bell pepper, parsley, and celery, stirring after each addition; cook until the onions are clear. Add 1 cup of chicken broth, stir to make a thick paste. Stir in the chopped garlic, the remaining chicken broth, and the beef broth. Stir in the okra, chicken, sausage, and Worcestershire sauce. Add Tony Chachere's Original Creole Mix, stir and taste. Add more seasoning, if you desire, according to your taste. Stir and mix well, reduce heat to low, cover and simmer at least 30 minutes to 1 hour. Serve over cooked rice.

Cooking Tip: If time allows, the easiest and most thorough method of removing fat from a broth is to refrigerate the broth until the fat hardens on the surface. The fat will lift right off.

Mary E. McCloud is a nurse and freelance writer. She and her husband, Scott, have three children and one granddaughter. They attend the Living Word Church in Greenville, Texas.

# Grammy's Dish

**by Sharen Watson**

*You turned my wailing into dancing;*
*you removed my sackcloth and clothed me with joy,*
*that my heart may sing to you and not be silent.*
*O LORD my God, I will give you thanks forever.*
PSALM 30:11–12 NIV

Where is it?" I asked, tears threatening to spill over at any moment.

Pots and pans rattled, banging loudly under the intrusion of my perusal, but I was determined to find the only piece of CorningWare I owned. It belonged to my grandmother for many years, and when Alzheimer's took her memory, it became a prized and sentimental possession. I didn't use it frequently, but when I did, I could almost smell the fragrance of sweet and sour chicken, one of Grammy's favorite dishes to cook. . .and one of my favorites to eat. Tonight I was preparing dinner in that same baking dish.

Yesterday I received a phone call at 3:15 in the afternoon.

"Sharen, there's no easy way to say this." I braced myself for the inevitable. "Grammy passed away this morning." Mom spoke quietly.

Fifteen years of Alzheimer's had taken her final breath, and I was determined to use the heavy, white baking dish to celebrate her life tonight. Grasping my treasure, I stood momentarily in silence.

"Are you okay, Mom?" my daughter asked from the other room.

"Yes," I answered. "Did you know that Grammy used to make dinner for me, in this very pan?"

"Really?" She smiled, comforting my grief with her caring presence.

"Chicken, rice, pineapple slices, and the sweetest sauce I've ever tasted. I wish I knew how to make it for you." I smiled, savoring the memory.

"What are you making tonight?" she asked me.

"Chicken enchiladas," I replied. It was one of our family's favored dishes.

The timer interrupted our exchange. The chicken was finished boiling and ready to shred. I set the beloved dish aside, mixed the necessary ingredients for the enchiladas, and added the chicken. My daughter watched me as I tentatively poured the mixture into the CorningWare, and I smiled.

In that special moment, dedicated to my grammy and my daughter's great-grammy, God taught me that cooking was more than just the preparation of a simple meal, but an act of love, embracing each of us with the fragrance of loved ones present and the sweet remembrance of loved ones gone.

*Father, thank You for precious memories of those who have preceded us to their eternal home with You. Thank You that You take our mourning and turn it into dancing—dancing with joy for our future home and reunion with those who have gone before us.*

## Chicken Enchiladas
Preheat oven to 350° F.
Cookware needed: 9 x 13-inch baking dish
(such as CorningWare)

Ingredients
2 cans cream of chicken soup
1 can cream of mushroom soup
8 ounces sour cream
3 cups shredded cheddar cheese
1 onion, finely chopped
3 large chicken breasts, boiled and shredded
12 flour tortillas (small size)

Directions: Melt butter in the pan. Mix all ingredients together except tortillas. When thoroughly blended, fill flour tortillas with mixture, fold, and lay in buttered pan. Top with leftover mixture. Bake for 45 minutes and let stand for 10 minutes. Serve with refried beans, tortilla chips, and Mexican rice. Garnish suggestions: salsa, guacamole, black olives, jalapeño peppers, and chopped onions.

Cooking Tip: Another option for families on the go: Boil, shred, and refrigerate the chicken ahead of time, or stop at the grocery store on the way home and buy a seasoned rotisserie chicken to shred into the recipe.

**Sharen Watson** resides in Spring, Texas, with Ray, her "most supportive" husband of twenty-three years. They have a daughter and two sons. Sharen writes short stories and allegories that find their root in the Word of God and is founder of the Words for the Journey Christian Writer's Guild. She is currently working on her first novel, dedicated to her beloved "Grammy."

# A Definite Stretch of Faith

### by Barbara Owen Haring

*Then the LORD said to Moses, "I will rain down bread from heaven for you. The people are to go out each day and gather enough for that day."*
EXODUS 16:4 NIV

While awaiting the return of my self-employed husband from his out-of-town job, I began planning how I would allocate the money he would be bringing home. This would be our first payday in over two months, and I was relieved that we could finally pay our bills. Upon his arrival, I knew immediately something was dreadfully wrong.

With great difficulty he told me that the job had not been properly funded, so we would not be paid anytime soon for the large construction job we had half completed. My hope plummeted, knowing that it could be months until we once again had an income. This would be a true stretch of faith. But I had yet to contemplate what this would mean for me personally.

The worst part of stretching my faith was realizing that I would have to cook every meal. It's not that I'm a bad cook—at times I even surprise myself with my prowess in the kitchen. Cooking just isn't an area in which I choose to apply my creative abilities. I rank cooking just a little above mowing the lawn on a hot Texas day. But, like it or not, I would be cooking. My stepson, Jason, was working for us, and being financially challenged also, he moved into our spare room. So, like it or not, I would be preparing meals for three adults—with no "visible" means to do so. Putting aside all thoughts of our shattered credit rating, I prayed for a miracle and concentrated on feeding bodies—and souls.

Over the next few months, I spoke often of the manna God had provided to His people in the wilderness and of the lad who watched Jesus bless his two fishes and five barley loaves to feed thousands of people. I marveled at the fact that we continued to have enough to eat, and we often had food left over.

It is amazing what can be done with eggs, milk, a box of Bisquick, and a little prayer. One of our favorite meals during this time was the "Easy Chicken Pot Pie" from the back of the Bisquick box. I double the recipe. It feeds two older folks and one very hungry young man quite well.

*God, You are great, You are good, and we*
*thank You for our food. By Your hand we are*
*fed; give us, Lord, our daily bread.*

### Easy Chicken Pot Pie
Preheat oven to 400° F.
(High Altitude: Heat oven to 425°)
Cookware needed: 9-inch pie plate

Ingredients:
1 2/3 cup frozen mixed vegetables, thawed
1 cup chicken, cooked and cut into small pieces
1 can condensed cream of chicken soup
1 cup original Bisquick
1/2 cup milk
1 egg

Directions: Mix vegetables, chicken, and soup in ungreased pie plate. Stir remaining ingredients in bowl until blended. Pour into pie plate. Bake about 30 minutes, or until golden brown. Serves 6.

Cooking Tip: Make sure your Bisquick has not expired. Not doing so can be a costly mistake, both in time and money.

**Barbara Owen Haring** lives in a small Texas town west of Houston with David, her husband of nearly twenty-five years. She works part-time for her husband's business. She is the mother of two, Andrea and Sean, and loves writing, reading, sewing, needlework, and current events.

# A Steamy Night in Georgia

**by Nanette Thorsen-Snipes**

*A man finds joy in giving an apt*
*reply—and how good is a timely word!*
PROVERBS 15:23 NIV

During one steamy Georgia evening, Jim, my husband, decided to fry catfish. I watched as he poured oil into the large frying pan and turned on the heat. Knowing him well, and realizing he might forget, I said, "Honey, remember it gets hot quickly."

"I've got everything under control," he said, then shooed the kids and me out of "his" kitchen. Satisfied that I'd done all I could, I returned to the Monday night movie. As Chef Jim waited for the oil to heat, he joined us. And we all became engrossed in the who-dun-it.

Soon David, my laid-back teenager, mumbled, "There's fire on the refrigerator."

Always the jokester, we laughed at him. Nobody moved as we watched the movie's mystery unfold.

A few moments later, David said with urgency, "Dad, there's fire on the refrigerator."

Only then did I realize David was serious, and what David saw was the reflection of flaming oil from the stove.

I jumped to my feet and raced into the kitchen to see Chef Jim's oil, ablaze beneath my kitchen cabinets. I screamed for help. Finally Jim and David raced in. Just as Jim began to put the flaming pan under the faucet, David shouted, "No! Don't put it under water. . . ."

Oblivious to David's words, Jim shoved the pan under the water. Flames leapt above the kitchen sink, licking at my new curtains with fiery tongues.

Jim did the manly thing and raced outside with the flaming yellow curtains and threw them to the ground where he stomped them to death.

Everything could have turned tragic that day in the kitchen when we didn't listen to my son. In the same manner, if we don't listen to God when He speaks, we may find ourselves tossed from the proverbial frying pan into the fire. The Word says, "Do not merely listen to the word. . . . Do what it says" (James 1:22 NIV). James was saying that if we remember what we've heard in God's Word and practice it, we will be blessed in what we do.

*Father, You say that when we pass through the waters, You will be with us and when we pass through the rivers, they will not sweep over us. Likewise, when we walk through the fire, we will not be burned, for You are the Lord God of Israel and You will ransom us. We thank You, Lord, that Your hand is always upon us no matter where we go.*

### Fried Catfish
Cookware needed: iron skillet

Ingredients:
Catfish
Salt and pepper
3/4 cup cornmeal
1/4 cup self-rising flour
Corn oil or peanut oil

Directions: After cleaning the catfish, sprinkle with salt and pepper. Place your cornmeal and flour in a paper sack. Pour 1 1/2 inches of oil into a deep, heavy skillet. Heat on medium-high. Drop 3 or 4 fish into the bag and shake gently, coating the fish. Place in hot oil and fry about 3 minutes on one side, then turn and fry 3 minutes on the other. If using fillets, you may not need to turn; just remove when they're golden brown. Place fried fish on paper towels to drain.

Cooking Tip: Never leave hot oil unattended. And never, never put flaming oil under a stream of water. Instead, turn off the burner and put a lid over the pan so there won't be any oxygen to feed the fire, and it will be quenched.

**Nanette Thorsen-Snipes** has published more than five hundred articles, columns, devotions, and stories in compilation books. Her stories are currently appearing in *Angels Where You Least Expect Them*, Publications International, Ltd.; *Heart of a Teacher*, Bethany House; and *But Lord, I Was Happy Shallow*, Kregel; among others.

# Feed Your Family; Feed Your Spirit

### by Gena Bradford

*I am the vine, you are the branches. He who abides in Me, and I in him, bears much fruit; for without Me you can do nothing. Every branch that bears fruit He prunes, that it may bear more fruit.*

JOHN 15:5, 2 NKJV

When I was a young mother, we moved into a small rental house with a plum tree in the backyard. The tree had hundreds of small branches loaded with plums. I was thrilled. I could make jam!

After picking the fruit, I cut into them only to discover that each tiny plum had a big pit. There were far more pits than pulp, and that batch of jam took hours to prepare.

A wise neighbor sympathized: "If your tree had been pruned to several main branches, your plums would have been large and sweet. All those sucker branches drain the life from the fruit."

Sucker branches! I realized that described my life. I was an unpruned tree. I had countless branches trying to feed numerous projects, as well as the responsibilities of raising a family and keeping a home. No wonder I felt tired and overwhelmed!

I prayed, "Lord, I am going in too many directions. I can't get it all done, and I don't know where to begin. Show me what is important to You. My life is bearing small fruit with big pits! Prune me, Father God."

I heard the Lord speak two things to my heart. He said, "Feed your family; feed your spirit."

My tree, now, had two main branches. I didn't know how all the other things would get done, but I obeyed. Daily, I began making prayer and Bible study a priority, along with menu planning and cooking nutritious meals.

There were days I didn't get my house clean or finish my to-do list, but with a well-fed family and my heart resting in the love of God, it didn't seem to matter. I knew that it would be a gift of grace whatever I accomplished as I trusted in Him. New strength and new peace blossomed for me from abiding in His Word and from giving Him all my cares in prayer. Life tasted sweeter.

God wants to nourish us in His love, and out of that fullness, we nourish the ones we love.

Feed and be fed.

*Heavenly Father, You are the Vinedresser.
How grateful I am that You've called me to
bear much fruit for Your kingdom. I want
to abide in Christ, the true Vine, and give
out of His strength and love. Thank You
for loving me and pruning me.*

## Jam-Broiled Salmon Steaks
Cookware needed: broiler pan

Ingredients:
Salmon steaks (3/4 inch thick)
Salt, pepper, garlic seasonings
Apricot/pineapple jam (or just apricot jam)

Directions: Preheat broiler. Place salmon steaks on grilling rack. Season the steaks with salt, pepper, and garlic. Baste with jam. Place the pan in the oven 5 to 6 inches from the source of heat. Broil for 5 minutes and then turn steaks. Baste with jam again. Continue to broil for 5 to 8 minutes. To test for doneness, see if you can lift out the central bone without bringing any of the flesh with it.

## Jam Thumbprint Cookies
Preheat oven: 375° F.
Cookware needed: cookie sheet

1 1/2 cups powdered sugar
1 cup butter
1 egg
1 teaspoon vanilla extract
1 teaspoon almond extract
2 1/2 cups sifted flour
1 teaspoon baking soda
1 teaspoon cream of tartar
Thick jam

Directions: Cream sugar and butter thoroughly. Beat in egg and flavorings. Sift dry ingredients; stir in. (Dough may be chilled and saved until later or proceed.) Using teaspoons, spoon dough onto greased cookie sheet, accounting for the size and the amount of the cookies you wish to make, and make a thumbprint impression in the center. Fill with favorite jam (up to 1 teaspoon). Bake for 10 to 12 minutes. Cool on cookie sheet for 5 minutes. Carefully remove from pan and complete cooling on rack. Frost with Powdered Sugar Frosting.

## Powdered Sugar Frosting

Ingredients:
2 cups powdered sugar
1 teaspoon almond or vanilla
2 tablespoons milk, approximately

Directions: Combine powdered sugar, almond or vanilla, and about 2 tablespoons milk. Mix until smooth and of spreading consistency. Yields: 26 cookies.

Cooking Tip: When making jam or applesauce, add half of a teaspoon of cinnamon to increase the flavor. It is delicious with any kind of fruit jam or fruit sauce/syrup.

**Gena Bradford** is a wife, mother, and grandmother. She enjoys the benefits of having fed her family and her spirit for thirty-six years. To her joy, her children are carrying on the tradition. Gena is a freelance writer. Her stories have appeared in various publications, including *Guideposts* magazine.

# Eating Is Believing

**by Laurie Klein**

*And while they still did not believe it*
*because of joy and amazement. . .they gave*
*[Jesus] a piece of broiled fish, and he. . .ate it.*
LUKE 24:41–43 NIV

It was an act of faith as unnerving as it was culturally sensitive: On our last mission trip, my husband, Bill, and I ate barbecued rat. Admittedly, we have since enjoyed shocking friends with our culinary daring, which may explain our recently braving the annual feast of our forefathers: the dreaded lutefisk.

Since Viking days, Scandinavians have soaked air-dried cod in caustic soda, then simmered the well-rinsed fish until the jellied mass wobbles. How I'd scorned this venerable dish at St. Olaf College, where rumor warned its vile aroma put folks in a coma.

Now, a friend claimed a new, stenchless recipe had made her a believer.

"No lutefisk," Bill muttered, as I double-checked her directions.

It seems the pungent, yuletide humidity of Lutheran lutefisk suppers haunted his youth, too. We couldn't remember eating it, though, so weren't we little better than bigots—we, the valiant, who'd eaten rat?

That did it. I bought one preprepared fillet. Eyeing the limp packet in the fridge, Bill quoted Elisha's company of prophets wailing, "There's death in the pot. And they could not eat it." I laughed, sound-biting Jonah: "And the Lord prepared a great fish."

Slowly, gingerly, I loosed the cod from its layered wrappings, thinking of Lazarus in his grave clothes. No smell. I rinsed off the lye, salted, then baked rather than boiled, it—and still no stink.

Didn't scripture state all foods were God's gift? Love it or loathe it, I would eat this entree. Clear my conscience. Across the table, Bill gave me that I-double-dog-dare-you look as I lifted fork to lips. I smiled. Neither gluey nor rubbery, it tasted mild, light, and buttery. Odd texture though, like fish jello.

Too often I give place to judgment, foreboding, and cynicism. Faced with the toxic stew of gourds, Elisha shook in a handful of flour, along with faith, and dished it up. "And there was nothing harmful in the pot" (2 Kings 4:41 NIV). May I do no less.

*Lord of the sea, keep my mind and heart open*
*to new cultures, tastes, and experiences. May*
*I accept all foods as presents from You, and in*
*good faith, feast in Your presence.*

## Lutefisk
Preheat oven to 400° F.

Directions: Purchase preprepared cod from the meat department at large grocery stores or Scandinavian specialty shops at Christmastime. Rinse well in cold water to remove lye. Cut into 3-inch squares and place in Pyrex (glass) dish (don't use metal pans). Sprinkle lightly with salt and bake (rather than boil) for 20 minutes, maximum. Serve with drawn butter, boiled potatoes, and lefse.

## Red Snapper
An afterthought: Here's a more user-friendly recipe.
Probably won't get many takers on lutefisk!

Directions: Soak fresh fish in milk (or thaw frozen fillets in milk) 15 minutes to 1 hour to reduce fishy taste. Rinse fish and press between paper towels. Fill metal pan with fillets, one layer thick. Sprinkle with finely chopped onion, salt, pepper, and dill weed. Cover with a thin layer of mayonnaise. Broil until golden, about 10 minutes. Serves 4 to 5. Serve with steamed veggies, drizzled with pan drippings.

# Norwegian Lefse

If possible, work (and nibble!) with a friend:
one person rolling, the second, frying.

Cookware needed: griddle (or several fry pans,
ungreased. If using fry pans, divide the
long roll of dough into 24 sections.)

4 cups riced or mashed russet potatoes
    (about 2 1/2 pounds)
1/4 cup heavy sweet cream or evaporated milk
2 tablespoons butter (preferable to margarine)
1 tablespoon sugar (optional)
1 teaspoon salt
2 cups all-purpose flour (approximately 1/2 cup
    per cup of mashed potatoes)

Directions: Boil and mash the potatoes. Add cream, butter, sugar, and salt. Beat until light, then add flour; mix well, roll into ball, and knead until smooth. Form dough into long roll and, if using a griddle, cut into 12 sections (24 if using fry pans). Form each section into a small ball. Roll out very thin with cloth-covered or regular rolling pin, well-floured, on floured, cloth-covered board or other surface. If needed, dust board with flour again when turning lefse dough. Brush excess flour from dough. Bake on ungreased griddle or fry pan at moderate heat until light tan spots appear. (Lefse browns quickly.) Turn and bake other side. Stack lefse on rack, covered with a towel, or between sheets of waxed paper to prevent drying while cooling. Store in refrigerator in plastic bags, or freeze until needed. Reheat lefse briefly in 400° oven. Cut lefse into halves or quarters and spread with butter, cinnamon sugar, or honey, and roll. Secure with toothpick. Crumbled sausage or brown sugar with sour cream are also tasty fillings.

Cooking Tip: Soaking fish in cold milk reduces fishy taste. Discard milk before cooking. Better yet, bless a neighborhood cat.

**Laurie Klein**, award-winning author of poetry, prose, and songs—including the chorus "I Love You, Lord"—has been published in numerous literary journals, anthologies, magazines, songbooks, hymnals, and sound recordings. She is co-editor at *Rock & Sling: A Journal of Literature, Art, and Faith*. Her forthcoming book of poems, winner of the 2004 Owl Creek Prize, is *Bodies of Water, Bodies of Flesh*.

Cakes, Cookies,
Puddings, Pies,
and a Moose?

# A Taste of Faith

**by Jenny Broughton**

*Oh, taste and see that the LORD is good;*
*blessed is the man who trusts in Him!*
PSALM 34:8 NKJV

In the spring of my eleventh year, I found myself in the kitchen of a children's home called a "cottage" in south Texas. On Saturdays, a few children would bake a dessert for the Sunday noon meal after church. This was a grand meal followed by prayer and Bible reading. All of these things were new to me, as I had been suddenly orphaned due to a murder/suicide.

It was my turn to help in the kitchen. Mrs. Dixon, my housemother, and I baked a pineapple upside-down cake in a skillet that day. I measured all the ingredients for her. I had never baked anything that I could remember.

I enjoyed watching Mrs. Dixon as she bustled about, getting the mixer, bowls, and beaters ready.

She was dressed in a simple housedress with a floral apron at her waist. I had noticed that the other children called her "Mom," and I wondered if I would call her that someday.

As we sifted the flour, she sang songs I had never heard of, but later I learned the titles: "His Eye Is on the Sparrow," "How Great Thou Art," and "I Know Whom I Have Believed." Mom Dixon enjoyed cooking, baking, and singing. She smiled, chatted, and invited me to taste or lick the beater and spatula.

At first it was bitter; but after "Mom" added vanilla and sugar, the batter became sweet and delighted my young mouth. Eventually out came a beautiful dessert. I had no idea those individual ingredients could produce something so beautiful and tasteful. The dessert was enjoyed by all of the children on Sunday.

After all my bitterness and loneliness from the loss of my parents, I realized through Mom Dixon's testimony of love in words, songs, and actions that God loved me. Eventually I learned to "taste" God and see that He had a plan for my life that was sweet and good. Just as I trusted Mom Dixon and had the faith to believe her recipe would bring forth a sweet dessert, I discovered that my days would become beautiful, too, when God turned my life right side up again.

*Lord, may each of us taste You and know You are good. May we trust You by faith to mix the bitter with the sweet in our lives to Your honor and for our good, so that we will enjoy the abundant life You have for us.*

## Pineapple Upside-Down Skillet Cake

(Mom Dixon's recipe is not available. This one is provided by Clema Broughton, Jenny's mother-in-law.)

Preheat oven to 350° F.
Cookware needed: large oven-ready skillet

Ingredients:

Pineapple Glaze:
4 tablespoons shortening
1 cup brown sugar
1 can sliced pineapple

Batter:
4 eggs
1 cup sugar
2 tablespoons water
1 teaspoon baking powder
1/2 teaspoon salt
1 cup flour
1/2 teaspoon vanilla

Directions: Heat shortening and sugar together in a heavy skillet until the sugar is melted. Cool. Arrange pineapple slices over the surface of this caramel mixture. In a bowl, beat eggs until very light and frothy. Beat in sugar gradually. Add the water alternatively with the sifted dry ingredients. Pour the batter over the pineapple. Bake about 40 minutes, or until cake is set. While cake is still hot, turn skillet upside down to release cake onto a serving plate. Decorate with cherries and whipped cream, if desired.

Cooking Tip: Measure all ingredients ahead of time. This saves time and steps. It will also tell you if you have all of the ingredients.

**Jenny Broughton** is a gifted communicator and conference speaker and advocate for children. She and her husband, Sam, have been in full-time ministry, planting churches throughout their thirty-plus years of marriage. Through humor and real-life stories, Jenny offers hope and healing.

# S'mora Chocolate Cake

### by Diana Wallis Taylor

*Be hospitable to one another without grumbling. As
each one has received a gift, minister it to one another,
as good stewards of the manifold grace of God.*
1 PETER 4:9–10 NKJV

There are as many recipes for chocolate cake
as there are cookbooks, from rich fudgy ones to
German chocolate with coconut. When I was about
fourteen, a friend of my mother's gave me a special
recipe for an, as yet, unnamed chocolate cake using
Hershey's cocoa. I was delighted with the pudding-
type frosting and the texture of the layers.

When my cousin Bud, who was in the navy, had
leave, he would appear at the home of some member
of the family, and we all took turns feeding him. One
day, I'd just made the chocolate cake when Bud arrived at our house. I gave him a piece and anxiously
waited for his reaction. He took several bites and

furrowed his brow. "It tastes like. . ." And then he beamed. "It tastes like s'more!"

Whenever Bud came to visit us he'd grin and ask, "Got s'more a that chocolate cake?" After that time it was always called "S'mora Chocolate Cake."

I realized in later years that he was often lonely and looked forward to the fellowship of family. Many times he would bring a buddy with him, the lure being homemade chocolate cake. As a young girl, unsure of herself, it made me feel special to be singled out for praise and to know there was one food that I did well which I could prepare for someone else.

Now that I'm older, I find it more difficult to find the time it takes to make the cake for family and friends, but when I do, I am still made to feel special for using my gift to serve them. It is time well spent. We sit around the table, eat cake, and laugh, and add s'more memories that are worth keeping. That must be what God had in mind when He created chocolate cake.

*Lord, cooking for family or friends is one way that we show our love and appreciation for them. Help me to put the thought into my offerings of food that make meals special. Help me remember that You are the unseen guest at every table.*

## S'mora Chocolate Cake

Preheat oven to 325° F.
Cookware needed: 9 x 13-inch cake pan or
two 9-inch round cake pans (greased and floured)

Ingredients:
1/2 cup shortening
1 1/4 cups sugar
2 eggs, beat thoroughly until creamy
1 1/2 cups sifted cake flour
1 teaspoon salt
1 teaspoon soda
1 teaspoon baking powder
1/2 cup Hershey's Cocoa
1 cup very hot water

Directions: Sift together dry ingredients at least twice. Cream shortening and sugar; beat in eggs. Add 1 cup very hot water alternately with dry ingredients to egg mixture. Bake in pan(s) 25 minutes.

## Pudding Rich Frosting

Cookware needed: stovetop saucepan

Ingredients:
2/3 cup sugar
4 level tablespoons cornstarch
4 rounded tablespoons Hershey's cocoa
1/4 teaspoon salt

WHAT I LEARNED FROM GOD. . .

1 1/2 cups water
1/2 teaspoon vanilla
1 tablespoon butter

Directions: Cook all ingredients (except vanilla and butter), stirring constantly. When it comes to a rolling boil, add vanilla and a walnut-sized chunk of butter (a heaping tablespoon); mix well. Cool icing slightly before putting on cake.

Cooking Tip: When making a cake from scratch, always use cake flour to make a more delicate cake. To substitute regular flour, remove two level tablespoons per cup and sift flour at least twice before using. I sift dry ingredients over a sheet of waxed paper, so that flour can be easily picked up and poured back into the sifter to re-sift.

**Diana Wallis Taylor** is the author of *Journey to the Well— The Woman of Samaria*. Diana speaks to women's groups on the changes Jesus made in the lives of women as she shares her testimony and her own journey to the well. She has received awards in songwriting and poetry from the San Diego Christian Writer's Guild where she is an active member.

# Chocolate Cake from the Heart

### by Bobbie R. Adams

*"Love the Lord and follow his plan for your lives.
Cling to him and serve him enthusiastically."*
JOSHUA 22:5 TLB

I grew up in a small east Texas town during the 1950s with Christian parents who were hardworking, loving, and caring. It was a time when mothers spent many hours in the kitchen preparing family meals as well as canning and preserving vegetables grown in their own gardens.

I, too, spent many hours in my mother's kitchen, preparing meals alongside my mother and grandmother. Often our work involved mundane tasks, such as shelling bushels of black-eyed peas, but what I enjoyed most was helping my mother bake cakes or cookies. We baked chocolate cakes and fixed fried chicken for church socials or for other special occasions or to take to someone who was sick or in need.

Not only did much work take place in the kitchen of our house but also it was a wonderful time of sharing thoughts, asking questions, and of growing for me. I learned many excellent homemaking skills from my mother, but more importantly, I developed and shaped lasting values such as patience, happiness, sharing, and love. These values have enabled me to cope with the loss of both of my children as well as other difficulties along life's path.

By acknowledging God in all our ways, we allow Him to direct our paths through the best of times as well as through difficult times. We know He is always in control, and because of this assurance, we can find peace and joy by serving Him.

Kitchens have changed in our modern life today. Microwaves and ready-mixes speed up the process of preparing meals. If I could influence young mothers with something I learned in the kitchen, it would be to take time to let children discover the steps of preparing daily meals. Let time in the kitchen become a place of teaching, learning, and letting God reveal Himself through His provision of daily bread. Food for the body is a necessity for daily living, but food for the soul brings eternal life. They can both be found in the kitchen of a dedicated Christian mother.

*Lord, help us understand how great*
*Your power is to help us when we trust*
*and follow Your plan for our lives.*

## White Chocolate Cake
Preheat oven to 350° F.
Cookware needed: medium saucepan,
three 9-inch round cake pans

Ingredients:
3 sticks margarine  (3/4 pound)
3/4 cup water
4 (1-ounce) squares white baking chocolate, chopped
1 1/2 cups buttermilk
4 eggs, slightly beaten
1/4 teaspoon rum extract
3 1/2 cups all-purpose flour, divided
1 cup toasted chopped pecans
2 1/4 cups sugar
1 teaspoon baking powder
1 teaspoon baking soda
1/2 cup flaked coconut

Directions: In a medium saucepan, bring margarine and water to boiling, stirring constantly. Remove from heat and add chocolate. Stir until chocolate melts. Allow mixture to cool; stir in buttermilk, eggs, and rum extract; set aside. Toss 1/2 cup flour with the toasted pecans; set aside.

Sift together the remaining flour, sugar, baking powder, and baking soda; stir in the coconut. In a large bowl, combine the dry ingredients with liquid ingredients; stir to combine. Fold in the pecans. Pour batter into three greased and floured cake pans. Bake 25 to 30 minutes or until a cake tester inserted into the center comes out clean. Cool in pans for 10 minutes. Remove from pans; cool completely on racks before frosting.

## White Chocolate Frosting

Frosting ingredients:
4 (1-ounce) squares white baking chocolate, chopped
1 stick margarine, softened (1/4 pound)
1 (8-ounce) package cream cheese,
    plus 1 (3-ounce) package cream cheese
6 cups sifted powdered sugar

Directions: To prepare the frosting, heat chocolate in the microwave oven until it melts; set aside to cool. In a large mixing bowl, combine the margarine and cream cheese; add chocolate and blend. Gradually add powdered sugar and beat until smooth. Spread frosting between layers, top, and sides of the cake. Serves 16.

Cooking Tip: Sift powdered sugar on plate before placing fresh cake on it to prevent the cake from sticking to the plate.

**Bobbie R. Adams** is a former hospital dietitian, home economics teacher, and businesswoman. The White Chocolate Cake recipe is from her cookbook, *Set Another Place. . . Company's Coming* (Wimmer Cookbooks, Nashville, TN).

# A Pot of Porridge

**by Wendy Dunham**

*A soft answer turns away wrath,*
*but a harsh word stirs up anger.*
PROVERBS 15:1 NKJV

Walking past the entrance to our kitchen, I saw my seven-year-old son, Evan, kneeling on a chair at our table. With one hand he held a wooden spoon and with the other he gripped the handle of our 3-quart Revere Cookware pot. And just the look on his face as his eyes caught mine told me he was up to something. Apprehensively I walked closer to get a better look. "Evan!" I exclaimed, my voice lingering between turbulence and repose. "What are you doing?"

"I'm just stirring up a new recipe, Mom."

"Oh, Evan," I said while looking at his two ingredients—a bulk-sized box of raisins and a whole slew of honey—"you need to check with me before you start creating! I've told you that before!" (This

175

wasn't his first offense of "creating" in the kitchen.)

I took a slow, deep breath and wondered how to react. Should I get more upset and angry, or should I respond in a loving manner? And as I recalled a recently viewed parent-teaching video by Gary Smalley (its topic was anger), my mind was quickly made up.

"Well, Evan," I said, "that's a very creative recipe. You know, it's almost lunchtime and I have nothing planned to eat. How about we finish 'creating' and use your new recipe to make something for lunch?"

Evan, both relieved and thrilled, shouted, "That'll be great, Mom!"

So with a bit of creativity, we added a whole lot of oatmeal, some water, a little milk, and a few shakes of cinnamon to make a very large pot of cinnamon-raisin porridge. Then when it was all done, and not too hot and not too cold, the Mama Bear (that would be me), and the Baby Bear (Evan, of course), sat down and ate their large bowls of porridge for lunch. . .and it was just right!

*Dear God, no matter what situation I may be in, please help me to always respond as You would, with tenderness, love, and self-control.*

# Fruit-Filled Baked Oatmeal Squares
Preheat oven to 375° F.
Cookware needed: ungreased 9 x 13-inch pan

Ingredients:
4 eggs (or equivalent substitute)
2 cups milk
1/3 cup water
2/3 cup oil
1 teaspoon salt
4 teaspoons baking powder
6 cups quick-cooking rolled oats
1/2 cup maple syrup
1 teaspoon cinnamon

Directions: Combine all ingredients. After all ingredients are mixed, pour into pan and mentally divide the pan into 15 squares—3 squares by 5. In the middle of each square, place 1 teaspoon of your favorite fruit preserves. Bake for 25 minutes. Remove from oven and let set until warm. Cut into squares and serve. Individual squares can be wrapped and frozen for future delicious breakfasts. Simply remove from freezer and warm in oven or microwave. Enjoy!

Cooking Tip: Always lick the beaters!

**Wendy Dunham** is a mother of two children, a registered therapist, and an inspirational writer.

# Looking Intently

**by Jacquelyn A. Kuehn**

*But one who looks intently at the perfect law,
the law of liberty, and abides by it, not having become
a forgetful hearer but an effectual doer, this man
shall be blessed in what he does.*

JAMES 1:25 NASB

I unfolded the small paper he handed me from his suitcase. "You can't believe how good Betty's Australian biscotti is," my husband said.

ALMOND BREAD, read the recipe's title. Only four ingredients—it looked easy.

"Thanks! I'll make it tomorrow!"

The next afternoon, as I scooped sugar, I noticed that Betty had marked "(1)" next to the measurement. I increased my quantity to match her adjustment. Then I noticed a similar "(2)" following the request for one cup of flour. In went two cups of flour.

Folding in the flour and almonds was difficult; it

was just too dry. I added a tablespoon of water, then another one. Finally I just ran water into the bowl until the dough came together. As the almond bread baked, my mouth watered from the warm fragrance.

Finally, I lifted a pale tan slice and bit down: The cookie was like a ceramic tile. Crunching harder, I managed to crack off one sweet corner. But I was thankful I had not cracked a tooth.

I turned back to examine the recipe. Suddenly I noticed two little instructional footnotes, numbered (1) and (2). Light dawned as I realized that the parenthetical numbers I had taken to be quantity adjustments were really footnote numbers. Because I had read carelessly, I was forced to toss the nut-studded tiles into the garbage.

How often do I skim carelessly over God's Word, just to be able to check off "Read Bible" from my to-do list, and jump into my day's work? Not only have I wasted time, but I feel as though I have read God's Word when I really have not. I end up with no help for my life that day, and I become conditioned to expect nothing from God when I read the Bible.

I am learning to look intently into God's Word to receive what He has for me and to obey what He tells me. When I read carefully, He equips and blesses me with useful tools for life. And when I obey Betty's instructions, the almond bread recipe works perfectly every time!

*Father, You have given me Your Word to equip me for life. Help me to read carefully and to listen to the Holy Spirit as He enables me to understand what You have for me each day.*

## Australian Almond Bread

Enjoy as biscotti, with coffee or tea

Preheat oven to 350° F.
Cookware needed: loaf pan

Ingredients:
4 egg whites
1/2 cup sugar
1 cup flour
1 cup whole almonds*

*Optional: You may also substitute pistachios or hazelnuts.

Directions: Beat egg whites until stiff. Gradually add sugar; continue beating until mixture is very stiff. Fold in flour and almonds. Pour into greased loaf pan, bake for 50 to 60 minutes. Cool in pan 15 minutes, tip out, and cool completely on rack. When completely cool, slice very thinly (1/8 inch); lay slices on cooling rack and dry in 300° oven for about 30 minutes, or until thoroughly dry.

Cooking Tip: Read the recipe all the way through before beginning to cook.

**Jacquelyn Kuehn** cooks, teaches music, walks with God, and lives with her family in the hills of western Pennsylvania. She says almond bread and God's Word are very, very good when handled correctly.

# My Chocolate Chip Cookie Lesson

**by Jane Rumph**

*It is better to trust in the LORD*
*than to put confidence in man.*
PSALM 118:8 NKJV

Still no brown sugar. I stared at the cupboard again, as though by my gaze the box I sought would materialize.

*I can't believe I didn't put brown sugar on my last grocery list,* my mind sputtered. Now late at night, my batter of chocolate chip cookies for tomorrow's party sat half finished.

*You idiot,* I berated myself. *You knew you were low on brown sugar after making cookies last week. Can't you keep a simple grocery list?*

Then another inner voice joined the conversation. *Calm down—it's not the end of the world. Besides, you can add molasses to regular sugar and it'll taste fine.*

As I mixed the batter using the substitutes, I

pondered my internal rage. Since childhood I've wrestled with a perfectionist streak. It has helped me be organized and capable but left me disappointed when others fall short of my standards. I lived by the motto, "If you want something done right, you have to do it yourself."

I could see, however, that this motto often betrays me. I've often refused help in fear someone else will bungle things. Consequently I neglect the mutual support of friends. Moreover, I tend to place unfounded faith in my own competence. Failure brings self-loathing, because the only one I trust let me down.

I slid the first cookie sheet into the oven, and the truth began to dawn. In my fallen humanness, I'm no more trustworthy than anyone. If I can do anything well, it's only by God's grace. And when I fail, I see more clearly that perfection and reliability come from God alone.

My thoughts turned to the brothers and sisters whose help I so often spurned. *Funny,* I thought, *if I learn to trust God to meet my needs, I might discover that those who are willing and able to serve are channels of God's blessing. And as I stop laying such a burden of perfection on myself, I might find it easier to live with my flaws.*

The aroma of fresh-baked chocolate chip cookies filled the kitchen, and as they cooled I sampled one. It tasted fine.

*Dear Lord, help me release my self-reliance.*
*Teach me how to put my trust in You—and the*
*ones in whom Your Spirit lives.*

## Chocolate Chip Cookies
Preheat oven to 375° F.
Cookware needed: cookie sheets

Ingredients:
2/3 cup shortening
2/3 cup butter or margarine, softened
1 cup granulated sugar
1 cup brown sugar, packed
2 eggs
2 teaspoons vanilla
3 cups flour
1 teaspoon baking soda
1 teaspoon salt
1 cup chopped nuts (e.g., walnuts)
1 package chocolate chips*

* For sweeter chips, use milk chocolate chips instead of semisweet. For more intense flavor, use dark brown sugar instead of light brown.

Directions: Cream together shortening, butter, and sugars. Add eggs and vanilla and mix thoroughly. Stir baking soda and salt into flour, then add to batter and mix well. Stir in nuts and chips. Drop dough by rounded teaspoonfuls 2 inches apart onto ungreased cookie sheet. Bake for 8 minutes, or until just set and starting to brown. For chewy cookies, remove from oven while still quite soft, allow to cool briefly on baking sheet, then remove to rack or paper towels to cool completely. Cookies will firm while cooling. Makes about 6 dozen cookies.

Cooking Tip: You can make an easy brown sugar substitute by adding 1/2 cup of molasses per cup of granulated sugar.

**Jane Rumph** is a freelance writer and editor from Pasadena, California. In addition to books that she has edited or coauthored for others, her own titles include *Stories from the Front Lines: Power Evangelism in Today's World* (Xulon) and *Signs and Wonders in America Today: Amazing Accounts of God's Power* (Regal).

# God's Stirring Passion

**by Sally C. Wood**

*You know when I sit and when I rise;*
*you perceive my thoughts from afar.*
*You discern my going out and my lying down;*
*you are familiar with all my ways.*

PSALM 139:2–3 NIV

For the past three years, I have entered a bake-off contest at my church. And for the past three years, I have won the grand prize at that contest! I am very proud of that accomplishment, and I love to refer to myself as the Bake-Off Queen.

But how did I get to be the Bake-Off Queen? Is it because I am extraordinarily gifted in this area of culinary expertise? Or is it because I spend hours and hours in the kitchen baking every day? No, it is neither of these things.

After much reflection, I realized that I was not winning the contest because I had been supernaturally blessed with great baking ability. As a single mom with a full-time job, there is no way I can afford the luxury of spending a lot of time honing the art of baking. In fact, with my busy schedule, sometimes it's all I can do to throw a meal onto the dining room table! No, the real reason that I kept winning the bake-off contests was because I had an inner desire to create something beautiful. A desire that emanated from within: a strong passion.

Because of that passion, I started doing my homework well in advance, months before the contest was even announced each year. I checked out numerous library books, clipped recipes out of magazines, and experimented with various techniques, constantly searching for the ultimate bake-off entry. I loved what I was doing, and as a result, I never gave up.

God has a passion, too—a passion and a love for each of us. And He never gives up on us. Rather, He continues to mold us, according to His glorious image, until we result in something beautiful that pleases Him.

*Father, we are a work in progress. Help us to continue to be faithful to You, never forgetting that You are the ultimate designer of our lives. Mold us and make us into something that pleases You.*

# Mrs. Peppers' Cutout Sugar Cookies

This is one of my favorite recipes,
because it is easy to make and yummy!

Preheat oven to 350° F.
Cookware needed: cookie sheets

Ingredients:
3 cups flour
1 1/2 cups sugar
1 teaspoon baking powder
1 teaspoon baking soda
1 teaspoon salt
2 sticks butter (1/2 pound)
4 teaspoons milk
2 eggs
2 teaspoons vanilla extract

Directions: Sift together first five dry ingredients. Using pastry cutter, cut sticks of butter into the dry ingredients until the mixture resembles cornmeal. (If you don't have a pastry cutter, use a potato masher.) Add remaining ingredients (milk, eggs, and vanilla extract) and stir until thoroughly combined. Roll out dough onto floured cutting board. Use cutters to cut out the desired shapes of your choice and place on ungreased cookie sheet. The cookies can be decorated before baking with assorted colored sprinkles of your choice. (Optional: Cookies can be iced after baking, then decorated with assorted colored sprinkles.) Bake for 8 to 10 minutes (or until slightly golden brown). Decorate as desired. Makes 4 dozen cookies.

## Cookie Icing

This is an excellent icing for cookies, but once you ice the cookies, decorate them quickly with colored sprinkles, because the icing hardens. (Then the cookies can be easily stacked.)

Ingredients:
4 cups powdered sugar
3 tablespoons meringue powder (can be found
   with cake decorating supplies)
1/2 teaspoon vanilla extract
Scant 1/2 cup warm water

Directions: Combine powdered sugar and meringue powder. Add vanilla and water and beat at medium speed until desired consistency is reached (5 to 7 minutes). Keep the bowl covered until you're ready to use the icing.

Cooking Tip: Don't let recipes boss you around— feel free to experiment! When the recipe asks you to mix nuts into the icing, try sprinkling them on instead. If your mixture seems too dry, try adding a bit more liquid. If you prefer pecans instead of walnuts, go for it. You are the baker and the creation belongs to you— if your new variation works, claim it as your own!

**Sally Wood** has a tremendous testimony of recovery from abuse. Her desire to share God's message of hope has launched her ministry through writing, speaking, singing, and comedy. Sally is active in Toastmasters and is a graduate of CLASS (Christian Leaders, Authors & Speakers Services).

# Food Is Love in Action

**by Sandra K. Bennett**

*Be not forgetful to entertain strangers:
for thereby some have entertained angels unawares.*
HEBREWS 13:2 KJV

**M**y wooden rolling pin is more than one hundred years old and carved from a solid piece of poplar log. It hangs in my pantry from a looped, tattered piece of homespun linen. For years it hung in Aunt Bonnie's kitchen, and when she was living her last earthly days, she passed it to me. Her grandpa, my great-grandpa Samp (short for Sampson), hand carved the rolling pin for his mother, Delilah. It serves as silent testimony to decades of communion between family and friends, and sometimes even enemies.

No matter who was at the house at mealtime, they ate. It didn't matter if a business deal had gone bad or the relationship had soured; if it was mealtime, feet were planted under the table. For the duration of the meal, a truce was called, and everyone shared blessing and nourishment alike.

There is an art to feeding folks, to getting a meal on the table. Women in my family know how to bustle our way around a kitchen and turn out a meal for eight or ten with little advance notice. The women in my family know a home-cooked meal is a balm in Gilead to a hurting soul. God has taught us how to heal with our food when our words fall short. In my family, the women have always more closely identified with Martha and not her sister, Mary.

The tradition continues at our Appalachian homestead, Thistle Cove Farm, where my husband and I have established a reputation for feeding anyone here at mealtime. There are times when we don't know the person's name when they sit down but are friends by the time the meal is over. We've met some lovely people along the journey.

I know the wrongs of the world cannot be righted with a meal, but it's a beginning. When folks are busy breaking bread, it's more difficult to break bones or speak unkind words. And breaking bread is a really good start.

*Father God, thank You for this food and the families represented at our table. Please bless everyone who shares our food and space. Help us pay our debt to others and give us strength to do the work You have set before us.*

## Thistle Cove Farm Shortbread

When life calls for food, I take a couple of quart jars
of homemade (is there any other kind?) Brunswick
stew, the best corn bread you'll ever have the honor
to eat, and my shortbread. No matter if sickness,
funeral, holiday gathering, etc., the
aforementioned combination is just right!

Preheat oven to 350° F.
Cookware needed: 8 x 8- or 9 x 9-inch pan

Ingredients:
2 sticks softened butter (8 ounces)
1 teaspoon vanilla*
1/2 cup light brown sugar
2 cups flour

*Optional: This recipe is very forgiving. In place
of vanilla, I've added fresh lemon zest and 1 teaspoon
lemon extract (my husband's favorite) or 1/2 cup
chocolate chips or 1/2 cup dried fruit or orange
zest or ginger. I've not yet finished experimenting. I
usually add and then taste; when I like what I taste,
I stop adding.

Directions: Cream butter with vanilla. I usually
scrape out a vanilla bean into this mixture, as well.
Add brown sugar and mix well. Add flour and mix
well. Pat this out into a well-oiled pan and, using
a fork, prick a star pattern. I use a pottery thistle

shortbread pan, thus giving this recipe its name. Bake for 25 minutes or until lightly brown around edges. Cool on a rack for 10 minutes and then flip out shortbread. Try to make this a smooth motion so the shortbread doesn't break into pieces.

Cooking Tip: Only real butter (not margarine) is used at Thistle Cove Farm, and when the stick of butter is unwrapped (if I've not churned my own butter), I use the butter on the paper as a lotion on my hands and face. If it was good enough for M. F. K. Fisher, author of *The Art of Eating*, it's good enough for me!

---

**Sandra Bennett** is Shepherd and Farmer at Thistle Cove Farm in the Appalachian Mountains of Tazewell County, Virginia. Dave Bricker, her husband, shares the farm, but not the farming, with assorted critters, beasts, and varmints.

# Sweet Mercy

**by Cristine Bolley**

*How sweet are your words to my taste,*
*sweeter than honey to my mouth!*
PSALM 119:103 NIV

Mom, can my college friends come here for our Bible study tonight?"

"Sure!" I answered. "I'll make sugar cookies for them." I knew my recipe from my friend Linda wouldn't fail me; everyone always raves about them. I thought I could be out of the kitchen before my daughter's friends arrived, but they settled in the adjoining living room as the last cookies were baking. I worked quietly but was pleased that I had a purpose for being in proximity to hear their discussions.

When they discussed the wicked servant in the parable of the talents, I waited to see if they discovered my favorite part of his story. Seeing they were missing it, I said, "Excuse me, there's a few minutes left on the cookies in the oven, then I'm out of here. But may I ask a question about this passage? We know that the master in this story is a picture of God, so do you think the servant was considered wicked because he was lazy, or because of his perception of the master?"

Looking again at the story, a young man read the idle servant's words in Matthew 25:24, " 'Master,' he said, 'I knew that you are a hard man. . . .' " (NIV). The young man who was leading the group said, "The servant didn't know his master, did he? God isn't hard. He wouldn't have punished the servant for failing if he had at least tried. God is full of mercy."

The timer chimed on the cookies, and so I realized my work in the kitchen was done. As I left the room, I was pleased by the grace that filled their final discussion. And before my daughter's friends left that night, they asked if I would lead their Bible study the next week!

Sure enough, my friend's cookie recipe hadn't failed me. They were quickly consumed at the end of the study. I used to think that cooking kept me from spending time with God, but my daughter's friends showed me that one way to the Father's heart is through the kitchen.

*Lord, give me courage to invest what You have given me to use, and bless the work of my hands to help others to see Your mercy and grace.*

# No-Fail Friendship Sugar Cookies
Preheat oven to 350° F.
Cookware needed: cookie sheets

Ingredients:
1/2 cup cooking oil
1/2 cup butter
1 1/2 cups powdered sugar
1 egg
1 teaspoon lemon
1 teaspoon vanilla
2 1/2 cups flour
1 teaspoon baking soda
1 teaspoon salt

Directions: With a mixer, cream oil, butter, and powdered sugar. Beat in egg, lemon, and vanilla. Sift together and add flour, soda, and salt to the batter, mixing until blended. Shape into small balls and flatten on a cookie sheet with a buttered glass dipped in granulated sugar. Bake 12 minutes or until done. (Don't overbake.)

Cooking Tip: Use a small ice cream scoop to make evenly shaped balls of dough.

**Cristine Bolley** is an inspirational conference speaker, author, and series editor for this line of special-interest devotionals from Barbour Publishing. Her mission is to launch new voices into the body of Christ and win the brokenhearted to Christ through stories of His grace and power.

# In Mama's Kitchen

**by Carolyn Brooks**

In Loving Memory of
Irene (Reese) Slaymaker Phelps

*Being confident of this very thing, that he
which hath begun a good work in you will
perform it until the day of Jesus Christ.*
PHILIPPIANS 1:6 KJV

Through Mother's kitchen door was the nourishment of our daily lives. Inside were all the necessary tools for the culinary expert—measuring spoons, measuring cups, grinders, choppers, blenders, and all sorts of cooking utensils. The sounds of mixing, chopping, and grinding filled the air. Sometimes the heat from the oven made the kitchen really hot, but the aroma signaled something great was about to delight my taste buds!

I discovered cooking was not without risk or injury. Sometimes I would cut or burn my fingers, but

Mother always had the right ointment, bandage, and comforting words to heal my wounded finger. She was a wise and skilled cook with precision accuracy on the necessary ingredients for her savory dishes. She knew her recipes well, and she compiled many of them by memory. Her eyes were her measuring tools, and she always knew how much of this, and how much of that was needed.

To capture her recipes, I had to empty each ingredient from her bowl and place it into my bowl. I then carefully poured each item into a measuring cup or spoon and recorded the measurement. But I still had to call Mother many times to go over recipes and verify ingredients. She always had time to talk with me and answer all my questions. When I followed her instructions, the result was always a success. If I made a mistake or altered the recipe, well, it did not taste as good.

So it is with a relationship with God, we must first enter through the door of Christ. Inside, we have access to all the right tools to equip our lives with success. God receives us just the way we are, with all of our raw ingredients. He knows what is missing and what is needed. He carefully adds a "little bit of this" and a "little bit of that." Trials and hardships often create the right temperature to mold and shape our lives. He desires that the sweet aroma of our personal experiences with Him will cause many to ask for the "recipe" and lead others to Him.

*Father, help me to endure when You*
*are blending the ingredients of my life to*
*Your perfection. Help me to trust You when*
*heated trials come my way. May the sweet*
*aroma of my relationship with You entice*
*others to taste the true riches in knowing You.*

## Homemade Banana Pudding
Cookware needed: large serving bowl

Ingredients:
3 eggs
1 cup sugar
1/4 cup cornstarch
1 teaspoon vanilla
3 cups milk
1 box vanilla wafers
2 bananas

Directions: Beat eggs and sugar in large bowl. Slowly add cornstarch and beat again. Add vanilla and milk and beat slowly. Microwave for 4 minutes and beat with wire whisk to remove any lumps. Microwave until desired thickness (approximately 5 more minutes). Line serving bowl with vanilla wafers (use approximately 3/4 box). Add thinly sliced bananas over vanilla wafers. Pour in the pudding mixture. Serves 6.

Cooking Tip: Cornstarch has a tendency to become lumpy while thickening in the microwave. Beat often with wire whisk to remove lumps.

**Carolyn Brooks**, Simply Divine Communications, is a dynamic speaker, author, and consultant. She is a member of the Professional Woman Speaker's Bureau and is a speaker with Christian and Professional Women's Clubs. Carolyn was a nominee for the Women of Excellence Award for her exemplary career and community involvement. She appeared on two nationwide television broadcasts, "Life Today" and "At Home Life," and is a coauthor of the book *Conversations on Faith* with Dr. Robert Schuller, Tony Campolo, and actress Jennifer O'Neill, and is also coauthor of *But, Lord, I Was Happy Shallow.*

# Looking in All the Wrong Places

by Therese Marszalek

*Then a great and powerful wind tore the*
*mountains apart and shattered the rocks*
*before the LORD, but the LORD was not in*
*the wind. After the wind there was an earthquake,*
*but the LORD was not in the earthquake.*
*After the earthquake came a fire, but the*
*LORD was not in the fire. And after the*
*fire came a gentle whisper.*
1 KINGS 19:11–12 NIV

While preparing a basil chicken dish for a special family dinner, I remembered a prayer petition from several months earlier. Expressing tear-filled disappointment, I told God that the answer He sent was not the answer I had looked for.

When I opened the cupboard in search of basil,

a neatly aligned spice rack greeted me. All bottles were lined up like soldiers, identical except for their contents. Scanning multiple rows of spices and seasonings, I found no basil. Certain I had the common seasoning, I touched each bottle's identification label with my fingertip, searching and researching each row. No basil.

Spotting a half-hidden bottle with no identification label, I thought, *Well? It's green. This will have to do for now.* Because of a pre-dinner time crunch, I could not afford a last-minute trip to the store. I sprinkled the mystery seasoning over the chicken, asking God to bless the meal in spite of the questionable adjustment I made.

Opening the same cupboard for the last time, I froze when I reached for the salt. There, in the front, stood a large bottle marked BASIL in sizable letters. Staring in disbelief, I could almost hear it announce, "Here I am!"

*How could I have possibly missed that?* I wondered. Three times the size of the other bottles, the basil made its presence known. But because I had been expecting a small bottle that matched the others, I missed out on the very thing that would have met my need.

Reflecting on the disappointment I had earlier expressed to the Lord regarding His answer to my prayer, I realized I had been looking only for the answer I wanted. But God, in His sovereignty and love, sent His reply in a package I didn't recognize. Knowing God is a faithful, loving Father, I smiled, knowing His answer was the best answer.

By the way, the dinner with the substitute seasoning turned out great. His grace covers us even when we get out of step with Him. After all, I did ask Him to bless my meal in spite of the substitute. And He did!

*Lord, help me to willingly accept Your answers to prayer, even when they arrive in a different package than I expect.*

### Frosty Chocolate Mousse

Ingredients:
1 1/2 cups whipping cream
1/2 cup sugar
1/2 cup sifted baking cocoa
1/2 teaspoon rum extract
1/2 teaspoon vanilla extract

Directions: In a mixing bowl, combine all ingredients. Beat until mixture mounds softly. Spoon into dessert dishes. Freeze for at least 2 hours before serving. Yield: 4 servings

Cooking Tip: Purchase hamburger in 3- to 5-pound chubs, precook it, divide into desired amounts, and freeze. This enables you to take advantage of the best price and saves cooking time when a quick hamburger casserole is needed.

**Therese Marszalek** is an author and inspirational speaker for women's ministries. Her books include *Breaking Out* (Publish America), *Take Me Off the Pedestal* (pending publication), and with Sheri Stone, *Miracles Still Happen* (Harrison House). Therese, her husband, and their three children live in Spokane, Washington.

# Love Never Fails

**by Mary Marcia Lee Norwood**

*Love never fails.*
1 CORINTHIANS 13:8 NIV

French Silk Pie!" I announced proudly to my husband, Ed. It was the first pie I made as a new wife.

With an embroidered towel from France draped over my left hand and my chocolate *"piece-de-resistance"* slightly elevated in my right hand, I entered the dining room with all the grace I could muster. It (the pie) looked splendid—*c'est magnifique*! No one would have ever guessed the battle I had preparing it—except perhaps for the telltale white flakes of flour I was still whisking from my hair and eyebrows.

The chocolate filling and the meringue were easy enough to make. But I fought the dough continually. . .adding more water, then more flour, then more water. . .until the dough was pliable. . .like clay. At last, I fitted the dough into the glass pie plate and molded the edges into a beautiful fluted design. (I was always better in pottery class than in the kitchen.)

As I pranced into the dining room, I fell! The French Silk Pie went airborne and then landed beside me. The white fluffy meringue disappeared into the plush then-popular 1970s shag carpeting. Chocolate was everywhere, but the dough didn't budge. It remained like hardened clay, glued to the glass pie plate. It looked good, but it would have broken our teeth if we had tried to bite into it.

I was the first to laugh. "I think I'll keep this crust and just add new fillings. It will save me the hassle of trying to make a new dough each time."

"I love you," my husband said as he helped me wipe up the mess.

Ed told his fellow firefighters about my French Silk Pie fiasco. One of them gave Ed a recipe for "Never-Fail Piecrust." I accepted the recipe from Ed because of the way he offered it to me: with love.

After thirty-three years of marriage, the piecrust recipe has never failed. More importantly, as Ed and I remain pliable clay in the Potter's hand, the love He gave us for each other never failed.

*Father God, Oh! You are the potter. We are the clay. You made us for a purpose, not just to look good, but so that our lives will carry the flavor of Your unfailing love to others. Keep us in Your perfect will.*

# Firefighter Ed's Never-Fail Piecrust
(This should make a double piecrust.)

Preheat oven to 450° F.
Cookware needed: 9-inch pie pan

Ingredients:
3 cups flour
1 1/2 cups shortening
1 teaspoon salt
1 tablespoon vinegar
1 tablespoon water
1 egg

Directions: Mix and chop flour, shortening, and salt together until flaky. Set aside dry mixture and in a separate bowl mix together vinegar, water, and egg. Add the second mixture to the dry mixture. Knead mixture, divide into two, and then roll out on a floured surface. Roll up the dough on the rolling pin, and then unroll it over the pie plate. Prick bottom and sides of pastry shell with a fork. Fill with your favorite fruit pie filling; or bake empty crust for 10 to 12 minutes, or until pastry is golden brown. Then fill with your favorite custard.

# French Silk Pie Filling

1 (1-ounce) square unsweetened chocolate
1/2 cup butter, softened
3/4 cup sugar
2 eggs
1 (4-ounce) carton frozen whipped topping,
    thawed (about 1 3/4 cups)
1 baked 9-inch pastry shell
3/4 cup whipping cream
2 tablespoons powdered sugar
Shaved chocolate (optional)

Directions: Place square of chocolate in top of a double boiler. Bring water to a boil. Reduce heat to low.

Cook until chocolate melts. Let chocolate cool. Cream butter. Gradually add sugar, beating at medium speed of an electric mixer until light and fluffy. Stir in chocolate. Add eggs, one at a time, beating 5 minutes after each addition. Fold in whipped topping, and spoon mixture into baked pastry shell. Chill 2 hours. Beat whipping cream until foamy. Gradually add powdered sugar, beating until soft peaks form. Spread whipped cream on pie. Garnish with shaved chocolate, if desired. Yield: one 9-inch pie.

Cooking Tip for Fluted Edge Pastry: Trim pastry 1/2 inch beyond rim of pie plate; fold under to make double edge. Use a knife handle to make the indentations. Use the thumb and index finger of your other hand as a wedge against the knife handle, working completely around the piecrust to make a scalloped, fluted edge.

**Marcia Lee Norwood** speaks and writes professionally about her life as a wife, mother, grandmother, and mother again in her fifties! Marcia and husband, Ed, have two adult, home-made kids, four grandchildren, and two chosen children: girls (both nine years old) who were adopted from China. God's presence in Marcia's life has turned ordinary circumstances into extraordinary adventures around the world. Her photos and writing have been published in newspapers, magazines, and books.

# Lemon Pie to Gladden the Heart

**by Sandra McGarrity**

*He makes. . .wine that gladdens the heart*
*of man, oil to make his face shine, and*
*bread that sustains his heart.*
PSALM 104:14–15 NIV

Her little boy rode our church bus. She had received the good news that she was carrying another much-wanted child. She and her husband rejoiced that their family would soon be complete. They hoped for a girl.

One Saturday my husband came home from visiting his bus route. His voice was tinged with sadness as he told me that the little family had lost their baby. "She [the mother] is devastated," he said. "Do you think you could make some food or something? They don't have any family living here."

Mike was a college student and we had two little girls to support, so I knew that the meal couldn't be anything fancy and definitely not expensive. I made a meat loaf and some vegetables. For dessert, I made a homemade lemon meringue pie, crust and all. It wasn't the easiest dessert to do, but I felt certain that the Lord was instructing me to make it.

When Mike delivered the food to their door, they were almost overwhelmed with gratitude. He had to make a second trip to the car to get the pie. As he approached the house a second time, the grieving woman burst into tears and said, "I know that has to be a lemon meringue pie. I have been craving it. It is my favorite; how did your wife know?"

Of course, I didn't know, but her heavenly Father knew, and He passed the word along to me, without my realizing it. Pie is a small thing, but it made her heart glad—and mine, too.

Our great big God cares so much about the little things that make us happy. His Word tells us that He gives wine to gladden the heart, oil to make the face shine, and bread to sustain the heart. All of these speak of things given for our happiness, not simply things given to fill our stomachs. He could stop at providing our basic physical needs, but our happiness means so much to Him that He gives the extra for our pleasure.

*Lord, thank You for caring about our every
need. I know that You are going to meet
those needs in my life today. Lead me to
that someone who needs a "lemon pie"
to gladden her heart.*

## Glad Lemon Pie

Give pie away, or keep to gladden your family's heart!

Preheat oven to 475° F.
Cookware needed: 9-inch pie dish

Piecrust Ingredients:
1/2 teaspoon salt
1 cup flour
1/3 cup, plus 1 tablespoon shortening
2 to 3 tablespoons cold water

Piecrust Directions: Combine salt and flour into
bowl. Cut in shortening. Sprinkle in water. Mix until
all flour is moistened. Gather dough into ball. Roll out
on a sheet of waxed paper, lightly sprinkled with flour.
Roll 2 inches larger than pie pan. Invert waxed paper
over pan and gently peel away, allowing crust to drop
into pan. Fold edges of pastry under and flute. Prick
bottom and sides thoroughly with a fork. Bake for 8
to 10 minutes.

Meringue Ingredients:
3 egg whites (keep yolks for filling)
6 to 7 tablespoons sugar
1/4 teaspoon cream of tartar (optional)

Meringue Directions: Beat egg whites until foamy. Beat in sugar, 1 tablespoon at a time. Continue beating until meringue is stiff and will form peaks. Set aside to top pie filling.

## Lemon Filling
Preheat oven to 400° F.
Cookware needed: medium stovetop saucepan

Ingredients:
1 1/2 cups sugar
1/3 cup plus 1 tablespoon cornstarch
1 1/2 cups water
3 egg yolks, slightly beaten (keep whites
    for meringue)
3 tablespoons margarine
1/2 cup lemon juice
9-inch baked pie shell
Meringue for 9-inch pie

Lemon Filling Directions: Mix sugar and cornstarch in medium saucepan. Gradually stir in water. Cook over medium heat, stirring constantly, until mixture thickens and boils. Boil and stir 1 minute. Gradually stir at least half of the hot mixture into the egg yolks. Blend into hot mixture in pan. Boil and stir 1 minute more. Remove from heat; stir in margarine and lemon juice. Pour into baked pie shell. Heap meringue onto hot pie, filling all the way to the edges of the crust. Pat with spatula to form peaks with curls. Bake for 10 minutes or until peaks are brown.

Cooking Tip: Although this recipe is neither easy nor quick, every woman should try it at least once in her lifetime. There is great pleasure in stirring the filling until it thickens and becomes clear. The bubbles that form and pop in the thick mixture are fascinating. Piling the meringue on top and patting it to make peaks with just the perfect curl is a work of art. There is something special about biting into a flaky crust that you made yourself.

**Sandra McGarrity's** writing has appeared in various magazines and anthologies. She is the author of two novels, *Woody* and *Caller's Spring*. She resides in Chesapeake, Virginia, with her husband of thirty-one years.

Baking for the Holidays

# The Palace and Pumpkin Pie Cake

**by Lynn D. Morrissey**

*Command those who are rich in this present world not*
*to be arrogant nor to put their hope in wealth,*
*which is so uncertain, but to put their hope in God,*
*who richly provides us with everything for our*
*enjoyment. Command them to do good, to be rich in*
*good deeds, and to be generous and willing to share.*
1 TIMOTHY 6:17–18 NIV

During the overwhelming pressures of writing my first book, my husband, Michael, and I escaped to a private piano recital in a thirty-five-room mansion, a stone labyrinth sprawled atop bluffs overlooking the Mississippi.

I thought this little excursion would offer soothing respite when I needed it most. Instead, I fidgeted in palatial surroundings, afraid to breathe, lest I collide with the abundance of ivory, silver, marble, and china that filled every cranny.

After savoring a five-course repast around an elegant dining table, I hesitated to approach the hostess, intimidated by her wealth and prominence. I wanted her recipe for Pumpkin Pie Cake, the luscious dessert I'd just enjoyed. She asked me to wait, then casually talked to her other guests. I found her delay annoying and wanted to leave but had no recourse but to remain.

After the final guest had departed, she invited Michael and me to her kitchen, took off her shoes, and set a teakettle to boil. She also sliced up more of the delectable dessert. We sat, sipped, nibbled, and chatted long into the evening.

Amazingly, instead of being intimidated by my hostess, I was captivated by her warmth and down-to-earth homeliness. I realized that I had wrongly judged her, assuming that someone who owned such opulence would also own a pretentious spirit. Instead, she was charming and generous, opening her home to share her possessions, talents, and time.

Now, whenever I make her scrumptious Pumpkin Pie Cake, I am amazed that such an extraordinarily easy recipe can yield such an abundantly rich dessert. And God reminds me of the gracious hostess who shared her simple recipe from the abundance of her generous heart.

butter. Bake for 1 hour 15 minutes, o
knife comes out clean. Cut int
squares. Refrigerate or serve w
whipped cream, if desired.

Cooking Tip: In th
are in season, cut off t
and use the shell
casserole conte

2 teaspoons cinna...
1 teaspoon pumpkin pie spice
1 3/4 cups granulated sugar
4 eggs

Topping:
2 sticks butter (1/2 pound), melted
1 box yellow cake mix (dry—straight from
    the box, unprepared)
1 cup pecans, chopped

Directions: Mix first seven ingredients in mixer, pour into ungreased baking pan, evenly sprinkle dry cake mix over mixture, then pecans, then melted

until inserted
preferred-sized
arm. Garnish with

e autumn, when pumpkins
heir tops, scoop out the insides,
as tureens for serving soup or a
its.

**Lynn D. Morrissey** is author of *Love Letters to God* (Multnomah), devotionals *Seasons of a Woman's Heart* and *Treasures of a Woman's Heart*, and contributing author to numerous bestsellers. She is a CLASS and AWSA speaker specializing in prayer-journaling and women's topics. She and her husband, Michael, have one daughter, Sheridan, and live in St. Louis, Missouri.

# Nannie's Rice Pudding Surprise

**by Viola Ruelke Gommer**

*Your hands have made and fashioned me;*
*give me understanding that I may learn your*
*commandments.*
PSALM 119:73 NRSV

The Thanksgiving table was cleared of the empty plates and serving dishes. Coffee, tea, and soft drinks were being served by my sister-in-law. The buffet was filled with dessert dishes, silverware, pies, and covered bowls with hidden delights. The apple and pumpkin pies were passed from the buffet to the main table. I stood at the buffet uncovering one bowl at a time, revealing its treasure. As I uncovered the second bowl, then the third, and finally the fourth bowl, I couldn't believe my eyes. What a surprise! There were four bowls of rice pudding.

I began to laugh. "You aren't going to believe this!"

My sister-in-law asked, "Why? What's wrong?"

It was clear that each of us had made a bowl of Nannie's rice pudding. We all laughed until we cried.

This was the first family Thanksgiving since my mother-in-law died. Nan always made the rice pudding for the family gatherings from an old family recipe. It appeared we all wanted to be certain that her rice pudding was a part of this celebration of Thanksgiving.

I asked, "What are we to do with all this pudding?" It was suggested that we taste each one.

Although each cook followed Nannie's recipe, the puddings were different in some unique way, either in flavor, or consistency, or color. Four cooks. One recipe. Four outcomes—all delicious in their own way.

What a life lesson! Nan's recipe taught me there is no need for me to try to be like anyone else. God has made each of us unique. He has made each of us special. We are a one-of-a-kind creation of God.

*God, help me to accept myself as a special child of Yours— fearfully and wonderfully made. Help me to celebrate the uniqueness of others.*

# Nannie's Rice Pudding
Cookware needed: large stovetop pan

Ingredients:
1 cup raw rice
2 1/2 cups water
1 quart milk
1 heaping cup sugar
2 eggs
2 heaping teaspoons cornstarch
1 cup evaporated milk
1 teaspoon vanilla
A sprinkle of cinnamon

Directions: Cook rice in 2 1/2 cups of water, cook until dry—about 30 minutes. Scald milk in large pot; add sugar to scalded milk. Mix eggs, cornstarch, and evaporated milk together. Add this mixture to pot of heated milk and sugar, stirring continuously. When mixture starts to boil, remove it from the heat. Add rice and vanilla to pot of mixture and place into large bowl. Sprinkle with cinnamon. Pudding will thicken as it stands. Can be served warm or cold. Add raisins if you wish.

Cooking Tip: Do something for the children. Do the kids like Oreo cookies? Buy chocolate cookies and vanilla icing. Give each child 2 chocolate cookies and a butter knife. Using the butter knife, allow them to make their own Oreo cookie: a chocolate cookie on top and bottom with the vanilla icing in between. It will bring smiles of satisfaction to their faces. Oh, don't forget the glass of milk to dunk them in.

**Viola Ruelke Gommer** is a retired nurse-educator and nurse-administrator. She is the mother of two, grandmother of six, and wife of a retired United Methodist clergyman. Vi has been involved in Volunteers in Mission in the U.S., Bolivia, Guyana, Haiti, Cuba, Zimbabwe, Dominican Republic, and Russia. Her spare time is spent in writing and photography.

# Grandma Hicks' Fruitcake

**by Don Dilmore**

*The end of a matter is better than its beginning,*
*and patience is better than pride.*
ECCLESIASTES 7:8 NIV

People who dislike fruitcake never tasted the kind Grandma made that is steamed for several hours before baking. As a small boy, I visited Grandma and Grandpa each Thanksgiving. Grandma always spent the following Saturday mixing fruitcake batter laden with nuts and fruits. She greased and floured the bread pans, which she had lined with brown paper, and filled them with the thick batter.

By this time we were asking, "When will it be ready?"

She answered, "Be patient."

After wrapping the tops of the tins in waxed paper and tying a string to fasten, she steamed the cake for three and a half hours.

We asked again, "When will it be ready?"

Her answer was always the same, "You have to be patient."

I watched her cut the string to remove the waxed paper and decorate the top of each cake with cherries, walnut or pecan halves, and candied pineapple. When it had baked for an hour, we were ready for a taste.

"No, children," she would say, "it's not ready. Be patient."

"We want to try it now," we would clamor, but she would smile, pat us on the head, wrap the fruit-cake carefully, and put it in the refrigerator.

Saturday evening and after church on Sunday we asked, "Can we cut the fruitcake now?"

"Be patient," she'd tell us. "It will be better a little later on."

Sunday evening after church, the fruitcake was finally cut. Our patience was rewarded with a mug of warm, frothy hot chocolate and a slice of fruitcake. The taste of those rich sweet slices was indescribable. Then we understood why she went through the lengthy process of mixing, steaming, baking, and cooling her delicious fruitcake.

My mother used Grandma's recipe for years, and now that Mom has gone to heaven, I bake fruitcake for the family, wrap it, and send it off to their homes. Marie and I enjoy our portion all year long. Stored in the back of the refrigerator, it gets better with age. God's way gets better with age, too: If we patiently wait upon His direction, study, and put into practice what He tells us to do, "the end of a matter is better than it's beginning."

*Dear God, help me to be patient with others,*
*with things I'm involved in, and*
*most important to be patient with myself,*
*knowing if I let You lead me, the end*
*is better than the beginning.*

## Grandma Hicks' Fruitcake

This recipe makes enough batter for four or five regular loaf pans. Read all the directions before you start. You may want to separate the eggs and heat the chocolate before you begin mixing.

Preheat oven to 350° F.
Cookware needed: four or five bread loaf pans, or angel food cake pans. (I always use a couple of small aluminum foil pans for any I want to give away.)

Ingredients:
1 1/2 pounds seeded raisins
1 1/2 pounds seedless raisins or currants
3 pounds candied fruit
1 1/2 cups chopped nuts
3 cups flour
3 teaspoons cinnamon
3 teaspoons allspice
3/4 teaspoon nutmeg

3/4 teaspoon baking soda
3/4 teaspoon salt
3/4 pound margarine
3/4 cup brown sugar
3/4 cup granulated sugar
9 eggs, separated
3/4 cup dark syrup
3 squares melted chocolate
3/8 cup lemon juice
3/4 cup orange or other fruit juice

Directions:

Step 1: Mix raisins, fruit, and nuts in a large pan. (The bottom of a turkey roaster works well.) Take 1/2 cup of the flour and sift over the fruit; stir to coat fruit and keep it from sticking together.

Step 2: Sift all the dry ingredients together except for the sugars.

Step 3: In a bowl, cream margarine and sugars.

Step 4: Add to the butter and sugar the egg yolks, syrup, and melted chocolate.

Step 5: Add the dry ingredients alternately with the fruit juices.

Step 6: Mix all of this with the fruit and nuts.

Step 7: Beat the egg whites until stiff and fold them into the mixture.

Step 8: Line the pans with brown paper. (It is easier if you cut the corners at angles. Let them overlap a little and then grease the paper quite thoroughly and shake flour around in pan until all the paper is greased and floured. Bang the edge of the pan to get rid of excess flour.) Pour in the batter.

Step 9: Take at least three layers of waxed paper wide enough to come well down over the edge of the pan and put over the top of pan, tying with string to hold it in place. I make a slip knot and lasso the pan and then tie it off. I wash the turkey roaster, put wire racks in the bottom, put about two inches of water, and put two or three tins of fruitcake at a time and steam for 3 1/2 hours. Be sure to add a little water as needed.

Step 10: Remove the paper from the top. Decorate with red and green cherries, nut halves, and sliced candied pineapple. Use your imagination and make it Christmassy. Bake for 1 hour. Put on racks to cool. Carefully unwrap, wrap in plastic wrap or waxed paper then in aluminum foil and put in the fridge.

Cooking Tip: Be sure to steam the cake for the required time. It's a lot of work, but be patient; and to paraphrase the scripture, the end of the batter is better than the beginning.

---

**Don Dilmore** is a full-time writer and award-winning author whose articles have been published in both Christian and general-interest publications. He has published three books, including a book for new Christians, called *New Beginnings*. His book, *Danny's Red Jacket*, won first prize for Young Adult Fiction at the Deep South Writer's Conference. Don teaches life principles through nonfiction, fiction, mystery, and humor.

# Grandma's Christmas

**by Vonda Mailen**

*An angel of the Lord appeared to them,*
*and the glory of the Lord shone around them. . . .*
*The angel said to them, "Do not be afraid.*
*I bring you good news of great joy that will be for all*
*the people. Today in the town of David a Savior has*
*been born to you; he is Christ the Lord."*
LUKE 2:9–11 NIV

Each Christmas, Grandma made decorated sugar cookies for all of the classmates of her twelve grandchildren. In November, she began baking hundreds of cookies to achieve her holiday mission.

She stacked the cookies, separating them by waxed paper, in airtight canisters. The aroma from her unique blend of lemon and vanilla flavoring filled the room as we popped the lids of her tins. It was amazing how fresh the cookies remained within these containers.

She organized her grandchildren into a production line of little elves, who were to dip Santa cookies into red icing and Christmas trees into the green icing without breaking them. (This was especially difficult, because we were allowed to eat the broken cookies.) As Grandma laid the cookies onto her paper-covered dining table, the enormity of the task unfolded. We had to work quickly once the pots of homemade frosting were poured into shallow bowls.

My little sister sprinkled tiny colored candies on Santa's bag to fill his pack of toys. I carefully perched a silver candy ball on each bough of the iced trees. As we worked, row after row of decorated Santa cookies and trees lay waiting for Grandma's final touch.

When the colored icing dried, Grandma piped white icing across Santa's furry hat. We were fascinated to see the tassel appear and the fur trim on his coat, buttons, boots, and belt materialize. She finished with a stripe of fur on his cloth bag to underline his toys. Then Grandma zigzagged a white ribbon across each tree so it looked like a string of popcorn had been carefully draped across its branches.

Each cookie was a masterpiece of carefully planned loved. Once completely dried, the cookies were wrapped in clear paper and tied with a pretty bow to be given to our friends.

Grandma's cookies were very popular on Jesus' birthday. She showed me that an act of love, a bag of flour, and a few cups of sugar can become a celebrated gift that causes people to remember the reason of Christmas long after the food has been eaten.

*Lord, thank You for the loving heart of a grandmother that lives to serve and bless others. Give me this servant's heart.*

## Nana's Chocolate Peanut Butter Cookies

These no-bake drop cookies are great for filling Christmas tins and giving away through the holidays.

Cookware needed: large stovetop saucepan

Ingredients:
2 cups sugar
2 to 3 tablespoons cocoa
1 stick (1/4 pound) butter or margarine
1/2 cup milk
1 cup chunky peanut butter
2 cups oatmeal
1 teaspoon vanilla

Directions: Mix together first four ingredients in a large saucepan and bring to a boil, stirring frequently. Boil for 1 minute. Then add peanut butter, oatmeal, and vanilla. Beat by hand until it the mixture starts to stiffen. Drop by spoonfuls onto an ungreased cookie sheet. Serve after the cookies harden.

Cooking Tip: Keep cookies in airtight tins for long-lasting flavor.

**Vonda Mailen** is a wife, mother, and grandmother whose short stories and poetry have had international distribution. Her award-winning poems have been featured in the Best Poems and Poets of 2002 and 2003. She is the Ministry Director of Peace Officer and First Responder Prayer Partners International, a mission that enlists prayer partners as intercessors for law enforcement, firefighters, military, and all first responders who lay their lives on the line to give peace and safety to others.

# Turning Up the Heat

**by Pennie Bixler**

*Blessed is the man who perseveres under trial, because
when he has stood the test, he will receive the crown of
life that God has promised to those who love him.*
JAMES 1:12 NIV

Candy making has always been a favorite holiday activity of mine, although I cannot truthfully say that it has always been a successful endeavor. Temperature is so crucial in the candy-making process. I have many memories of beautiful caramels, fluffy divinity, and fudge that melts in your mouth. I also have threatened to throw out expensive cookware because the sweet confection has been cooked too long or was not stirred enough and has cemented itself onto the side of the pan.

God recently showed me that making homemade candy is a great parallel to the way we can behave in the midst of trials. We feel the heat the trial brings. He longs for us to let His Spirit stir us up. He wants us to trust the direction He takes us. He wants to show us that we can become different. Just as the liquid ingredients of our candy can take on a different form, our character is formed by the combination of the heat and His stirring.

We can allow ourselves to be stirred up by God's Spirit and trust that He is doing what must be done in order to make us sweeter in the process. Or we can refuse to be stirred and become hard and crusty because of the heat we feel. So often I have adhered myself to what is familiar instead of allowing myself to be stirred. I have fought the direction I am being led. I am most certain that I've also left a bad taste in others' mouths. I had not become sweeter or better. Most importantly, I had not become what God had intended for me to become.

I am getting much better at recognizing that heat is good. I see myself coming out as that perfect confection—sweeter because of the process. God is doing amazing things in my life, and weathering His stirring is so much easier than holding on to the familiar and resisting the leading of His Spirit.

My candy-making is much better, also! I guess in both cases—in candy and character—practice makes perfect!

*Lord, I pray that You use my trials to make me
sweeter. Change my character into a greater
likeness of Yourself, and help me to remember
to let go of the side of my pan. Help me to
recognize the stirring of Your Spirit, so that I
may go in any direction You turn me. Thank
You for caring so much about me in order to
make me Your sweet confection.*

## Divinity
(Makes a great Christmas gift!)

Cookware needed: saucepan, 9 x 13-inch pan

Ingredients:
2 egg whites, stiffly beaten
2 2/3 cups sugar
2/3 cup light corn syrup
1/2 cup water
1 teaspoon vanilla
2/3 cup broken walnuts

Directions: Beat the egg whites until stiff; set
aside. Mix sugar, corn syrup, and water in saucepan.
Stir over low heat until sugar is dissolved; then cook
(without stirring) to 260° until mixture reaches the
hard-ball state. (Note: To determine hard-ball stage,
drop a little into cold water and it should form a hard
ball). Remove from heat and pour, beating constantly, in a fine stream into the beaten egg whites. Add

vanilla and continue beating until mixture holds its shape and becomes slightly dull. Fold in nuts. Spread in a greased pan with a spoon or spatula coated with vegetable cooking spray. Cut into 1-inch squares when firm. Makes 48 pieces.

Cooking Tip: When cooling candy, make sure that it is in a place that it will not be shaken or disturbed in any way. Do not stir or bump the dish.

**Pennie Bixler** is wife of Mike and mom to Aaron and Bridgette. She is also a freelance writer, speaker for women's conferences, and director of SAHMmies, a ministry for stay-at-home moms. She enjoys showing moms how to realize their full potential through biblical teaching.

# Where There Is Always Room

**by Karen Sackett**

*"In My Father's house are many dwelling places;
if it were not so, I would have told you; for I go
to prepare a place for you. And if I go and prepare a
place for you, I will come again, and receive you to
Myself; that where I am, there you may be also."*
JOHN 14:2–3 NASB

She wore a crown of silver braids and over her blue print dress, a clean white apron—her ruffled royal mantle. She carried before her a plate of soft warm fudge cookies, and the enticing aroma of chocolate and cinnamon wafted ahead to herald her entrance. Bringing her gift to honor Jesus on Christmas, Aunt Sue was not unlike a modern female version of one of the three kings. That is how I remember her.

It is not only the memory of her sweet smile and gentle nature that makes her cookie recipe a treasured heirloom; there was one more thing about Aunt Sue.

She was not really my aunt—if you count genetics or marriage. In fact, she had no family at all when she came to live in the little apartment located at the end of the grape arbor behind my grandparents' house.

She was in her sixties when she moved in; soft-spoken and kind, it did not take long for her to become "Aunt" Sue. From the beginning, she was included in all family activities, large and small; we would have missed so much without her. She touched us all with her warmth, love, and quiet dignity—not to mention her fudge cookies!

But what if, like the innkeeper in Bethlehem over two thousand years ago, Grandma and Grandpa had decided that there was no room for another person in their hearts, at the table, or in their small home? It would have been justified, certainly. With Grandma and Grandpa's eight grown children and their families, various friends, neighbors, cousins, and second cousins, there were so many of us at family gatherings that counting us all was impossible.

But thankfully, like the manger in Bethlehem, there was always room for one more. I am glad that heaven is like that.

*Dear Lord, I am so thankful that You made sure that there is room at Your table for everyone. I also rejoice that You have even prepared a place for me and for all who choose to come!*

## Aunt Sue's Fudge Cookies

These are surprisingly light for being called a fudge cookie.

Preheat oven to 350° F.
Cookware needed: cookie sheets

Ingredients:
1/2 cup shortening
3/4 cup brown sugar, packed
1/4 cup granulated sugar
1 egg
1 1/2 cups flour
1/3 cup cocoa powder (unsweetened baking cocoa)
1 teaspoon baking soda
1/4 teaspoon salt
2 to 3 teaspoons ground cinnamon
1/2 cup canned evaporated milk (not sweetened condensed milk)

Directions: Cream shortening, sugars, and egg until fluffy. Set bowl aside. Sift together the remaining dry ingredients. Add sifted ingredients alternately with the 1/2 cup canned evaporated milk. Mix well. Drop by tablespoon onto ungreased cookie sheet. Bake 12 to 14 minutes. Makes about 2 to 3 dozen.

While these cookies are wonderful the way Aunt Sue made them over sixty years ago, through the years I have tried the following variations. (I think she would approve.)

Variation 1: Add 2 generous tablespoons crushed chocolate-covered espresso beans to batter.

Variation 2: Add 1 generous tablespoon grated orange peel—fresh or dried.

Variation 3: Add up to 1/4 cup finely snipped dried apricots or dried cherries.*

Variation 4: Hold the cinnamon and add 1 teaspoon almond flavoring plus 1 rounded tablespoon toasted ground almonds.

Variation 5: Hold the cinnamon and add 1 crushed small candy cane. You may also want to add 1 teaspoon mint flavoring if you want more mint flavor.

*Cooking Tip: When snipping dried fruit into small pieces, rub a small amount of cooking oil on the blades of your kitchen shears to keep them from gumming up.

**Karen Sackett**, her husband, John, and their five cats live in Montana and share a forest with an assortment of other animals. God has given her a passion for sharing His grace, especially through her writing and old-time gospel music.

# Messy Recipe Cards

**by Barb Loftus Boswell**

*Just then a woman who had been subject to bleeding
for twelve years came up behind him and touched the
edge of his cloak. She said to herself, "If I only touch his
cloak, I will be healed." Jesus turned and saw her. "Take
heart, daughter," he said, "your faith has healed you."
And the woman was healed from that moment.*
MATTHEW 9:20–22 NIV

Cleaning up from my Christmas baking, I
noticed the splattered ingredients on the well-worn
recipe cards. *What a mess!* I thought for a moment,
but then realized that their state of untidiness was a
direct result of their usefulness. Some of my other
recipe cards remain quite pristine; they never come
out of the box!

The same is true of my books. It's easy to tell
the much-read and used ones; they are the ones with
pages that are rumpled and dog-eared. How much

fonder I am of those, though, than the untouched books in their shiny new covers!

It occurred to me that God often calls us to get a little messy in order to be useful to Him. What good are we to His work if we remain in our "boxes"? He may even need us to be worn and dog-eared for His service.

Jesus touched the untouchables of His day—the lepers, the prostitutes, and the tax collectors. The woman who bled for twelve years was considered "unclean" by their Jewish law. She was to be avoided. Yet Jesus did not rebuke her for touching Him (an act that would render Him unclean). He healed her and restored her in society's eyes.

He calls us to be His hands and feet today. We can choose to stay clean and unsoiled—and probably never impact a life for the Lord—or we can be the "friend of sinners" that Jesus was.

*Father God, forgive me for fearing to dirty my hands with Your work. Lord, use me in Your kingdom, for Your service. Move me out of my comfortable, clean box to be used by You! Lead me in Your ways, Lord Jesus. It's in Your name I pray, amen.*

## Sweet Potato Casserole
A great addition to any holiday meal!

Preheat oven to 400° F.
Cookware needed: 8 x 8-inch glass baking dish

Ingredients:
1 large can sweet potatoes, drained, about 3 cups
1/2 cup sugar
1/2 cup orange juice
2 eggs
1 teaspoon vanilla

Topping ingredients:
1/4 cup butter
1 cup brown sugar
1/2 cup flour
Pinch of cinnamon
1 cup chopped, toasted pecans

Directions: Combine first five ingredients. Pour into ungreased pie plate or 8x8-inch glass pan (9x13-inch if you double the recipe). For topping: Melt butter and add remaining ingredients (will be dry and crumbly). Sprinkle on top of sweet potato mixture and bake for 30 minutes (40 minutes, if doubled).

Cooking Tip: When measuring sticky ingredients such as shortening or peanut butter, line the measuring cup with plastic wrap. The ingredients will be easy to add to the recipe, with no messy scraping or cleanup.

**Barbara Loftus Boswell** is a freelance writer and abstinence educator. She has written for *Chicken Soup for the Bride's Soul* and *But, Lord, I Was Happy Shallow.*

# Cris's Cooking Tip

I hope that after reading these stories, you will see your time in the kitchen as an opportunity to draw near to God and celebrate the people in your life. Remember, the best recipes are the ones that inspire people to come back again for s'more—more fun, more fellowship, and more satisfaction for the longing we have to connect with each other and with God.

My mother was a working mom, and we ate out a lot, but I remember almost every meal that she cooked at home. No one could make vegetable soup, baked ham, scalloped potatoes, or chocolate sour-cream cake with caramel icing that tasted like hers. When I miss her, I make her vegetable soup or something else from the recipe book she left to me.

Most everyone has good feelings attached to some favorite food they enjoyed, because taste (which is related to smell) is the strongest of our five senses to trigger nostalgic memories. That is why certain foods help us to remember days that are worth celebrating.

I believe that is why God chose to use food to help us remember important moments of our spiritual history. The Passover meal with lamb and bitter herbs helped His people remember how the blood of the lamb on their doorposts caused death to pass over them when He set them free from the bitter bondage of slavery. Now the bread and wine of Communion remind us that His Son's blood was shed as the sacrificial lamb for our sins, and His body was broken for our eternal redemption. Jesus said, "I am the living bread that came down from heaven. If anyone eats of this bread, he will live forever. This bread is my flesh, which I will give for the life of the world" (John 6:51 NIV).

The Bible has a great deal to say about food—if it weren't for hunger, we might never seek God, who promises to give us our daily bread. No wonder He designed us for six small meals a day just to keep our metabolism functioning. Jesus said, "It is my Father who gives you the true bread from heaven. For the bread of God is he who comes down from heaven and gives life to the world. . . . I am the bread of life. He who comes to me will never go hungry, and he who believes in me will never be thirsty" (John 6:32–33, 35 NIV).

If you've never trusted your life to God's recipe for living the abundant life, I encourage you to simply pray:

> *Lord, I can see by the stories of people who know You, that You want to be intimately involved in our lives. I give You all the ingredients of my life and trust its outcome to Your divine ability to make something good of it. Fill me with Your living water and feed me*

*with Your daily bread so that my faith
in You will grow. I pray that Your will be
done in my life; forgive me for hurting
others, as I forgive them for hurting me;
and lead me not into temptation, but
deliver me from evil all the days of my life.
I ask these things in Jesus' name, amen.*

# About the Editor

Cristine Bolley is an author, editor, and inspirational speaker who has written several books in addition to this popular devotional series. She draws practical life-lessons from her experience as a wife, mother of three daughters, grandmother, and her encounters with God. Her message is, "God has a good purpose for your life, provision for your needs, a plan for getting you to the place you need to be, and the power to keep you safe along the way." Her desire is to explain the grace and power of God's truth with clarity to empower people to live the abundant life His Word promises we can have.

For more information about her conference workshops and books, write to:

Cristine Bolley
Wings Unlimited
P.O. Box 691532
Tulsa, OK 74169-1532

# ALSO AVAILABLE FROM BARBOUR PUBLISHING

### What I Learned from God While Quilting
*by Ruth McHaney Danner and Cristine Bolley*
Includes true stories on a quilting theme, followed by a spiritual application, a brief prayer, and a practical quilting tip.
224 pages.

1-59310-014-0

### Prayers and Promises for Women
*by Toni Sortor*
Puts biblical guidance at the reader's fingertips, through 200 carefully selected verses—categorized into 50 relevant topics—each accompanied by a contemporary prayer.
224 pages.

1-58660-832-0

### A Gentle Spirit
*by Ashleigh Bryce Clayton*
Emphasizing spiritual growth and personal development, this popular daily devotional draws upon the best writing of contemporary and classic Christian women.
384 pages.

1-57748-503-3

## Wherever Books Are Sold